# Between Real and Ideal

**UNC** | COLLEGE OF ARTS AND SCIENCES
Germanic and Slavic Languages and Literatures

From 1949 to 2004, UNC Press and the UNC Department of Germanic & Slavic Languages and Literatures published the UNC Studies in the Germanic Languages and Literatures series. Monographs, anthologies, and critical editions in the series covered an array of topics including medieval and modern literature, theater, linguistics, philology, onomastics, and the history of ideas. Through the generous support of the National Endowment for the Humanities and the Andrew W. Mellon Foundation, books in the series have been reissued in new paperback and open access digital editions. For a complete list of books visit www.uncpress.org.

# Between Real and Ideal
The Course of Otto Ludwig's Development as a Narrative Writer

WILLIAM H. MCCLAIN

UNC Studies in the Germanic Languages and Literatures
Number 40

Copyright © 1963

This work is licensed under a Creative Commons CC BY-NC-ND license. To view a copy of the license, visit http://creativecommons.org/licenses.

Suggested citation: McClain, William H. *Between Real and Ideal: The Course of Otto Ludwig's Development as a Narrative Writer*. Chapel Hill: University of North Carolina Press, 1963. DOI: https://doi.org/10.5149/9781469657936_McClain

Library of Congress Cataloging-in-Publication Data
Names: McClain, William H.
Title: Between real and ideal : The course of Otto Ludwig's development as a narrative writer / by William H. McClain.
Other titles: University of North Carolina Studies in the Germanic Languages and Literatures ; no. 40.
Description: Chapel Hill : University of North Carolina Press, [1963] Series: University of North Carolina Studies in the Germanic Languages and Literatures. | Includes bibliographical references.
Identifiers: LCCN 63063586 | ISBN 978-0-8078-8040-1 (pbk: alk. paper) | ISBN 978-1-4696-5793-6 (ebook)
Subjects: Ludwig, Otto, 1813-1865.
Classification: LCC PD25 .N6 NO. 40 | DCC 833/ .7

*To Ernst Feise and Harold Jantz*

## CONTENTS

INTRODUCTION.................................. 1
CHAPTER I     THE DECISION TO BECOME A WRITER. *DAS HAUSGESINDE* ................... 8
CHAPTER II    A PARODY. *DIE EMANZIPATION DER DOMESTIKEN*.................... 13
CHAPTER III   A FAIRY-TALE FROM EVERYDAY LIFE. *DIE WAHRHAFTIGE GESCHICHTE VON DEN DREI WÜNSCHEN*..................... 21
CHAPTER IV    THE TURNING-POINT. *MARIA* .......... 30
CHAPTER V     *DIE BUSCHNOVELLE* AND THE PROSE FRAGMENTS.................... 38
CHAPTER VI    TWO SCENES FROM PROVINCIAL LIFE. *DIE HEITERETEI* AND *AUS DEM REGEN IN DIE TRAUFE*...................... 44
CHAPTER VII   *ZWISCHEN HIMMEL UND ERDE*.......... 57
CHAPTER VIII  FROM PRACTICE TO THEORY. *DIE ROMANSTUDIEN* ..................... 69
CONCLUSION.................................... 79
NOTES ........................................ 88
LIST OF WORKS CONSULTED ...................... 98
INDEX ........................................ 106

# INTRODUCTION

Although Otto Ludwig's highest aspiration throughout his life was to become a great dramatist, at an early point in his career he became convinced that the various narrative art forms were far more suitable than the drama for representing the complex reality of his own day. At one point in his *Romanstudien* he even goes so far as to speak of his own age as being an "epic" age.[1] In this context, to be sure, the term is not employed in its conventional sense. Here it means not an heroic age, but one in which outer reality impinges on human life and activity to such a degree that it seriously hampers freedom of choice and freedom of action. The term "dramatic" is used in the same restrictive way in the passage to designate the opposite kind of age, that is, one in which people enjoy freedom of the will to the point of being able to act more or less as free agents. As his example of a "dramatic" age he cites the period of Shakespeare, and for his example of an "epic" age he chooses the period of antiquity in which men were still subject to the whims of the gods and both men and gods were subject to the whims of fate. The degree to which outer reality affected the lives of his contemporaries caused him to think of his own age, too, as "epic" in this special sense; and because of this he felt that narrative art forms, which allow so many more possibilities for depicting the external conditions and influences which shape the course of human life, were the ideal media for representing contemporary reality.[2]

Because Ludwig drew a distinction between epic and dramatic art in his critical writings several studies have concerned themselves, as mine does, with his narrative works only. With one exception, however, most of these have been discussions of individual stories or of special aspects of his work as a writer of fiction.[3] Mine is a comprehensive study. I have sought to accomplish in it two things in the main. My first aim was to provide, in light of recent scholarship and from the point of view of modern critical methods, an account of Ludwig's achievement as a writer of fiction and as a critic of the novel. Since he occupied such a uniquely representative position, however, both as a creative writer and as the critic who first gave currency to the term "poetischer Realismus," my study has also become an account of the evolution which took place in German fiction and in the theory of the novel during the period of literary realism. It might thus be said to move on two levels and to fulfill a double function in the sense that it answers both specific questions concerning Ludwig's contribution to the development of realism in German fiction and the broader one concerning the significance of his work as a kind of epitome of the movement as a whole in Germany between 1830 and 1865.

Since my main concern was to show the stages by which Ludwig developed from a clumsy beginner to a narrative writer of great skill I had to take all of his prose writings into account. My approach was to regard each as a little world created by him. This meant looking closely at the structure of each. By "structure" I mean here both the sum total of the elements of which each is made and the final shape of each, that is, the form which makes each what it is as distinct from all others. Because the form of a narrative work, unlike that of a painting or a piece of sculpture, is something which constantly eludes us, the best means of gaining an impression of the formal structure of Ludwig's stories seemed that of reconstructing, insofar as this was possible, the process by which they had come into being. To do this I began with the original sketches and observed how he built the final structures, sentence by sentence, paragraph by paragraph.

To measure his progress I attempted to discover the stages by which he learned to fit together the structural elements of a story in such a way as to produce on the mind and imagination of the reader a sense of harmony and coherence. In evaluating his achievement from this point of view I followed the prompting of Ludwig himself, in a sense, for he believed, as we know from his critical writings, that both the authenticity and the all-important aesthetic appeal of a literary work depend mainly on the orderly arrangement of its parts. Since our feeling of the authenticity of a literary work also depends on the kind of experiences it offers us and the kind of people we meet in it, however, I also paid close attention to characterization, the composition of individual scenes, the manner of handling temporal and spatial relations, and narrative style in considering the stories as worlds.

By reading Ludwig's narrative works in this way I was able to perceive, in what had at first seemed a heterogeneous collection of tales and fragments of tales, a consistent pattern of development which indicates that from the beginning Ludwig was moving in a new and independent direction as a writer of fiction. Since one can best measure what is new in a writer's attitudes and techniques by comparing them with earlier ideas about the relationship between art and reality and earlier methods of representing reality in art,

I found it necessary to look constantly to the past as I went along. And because Ludwig's *Romanstudien* contain all of his ideas on the ways of telling a story and all of his thoughts about tempo, suspense, characterization, form, and other technical matters, I also turned to these from time to time. This seemed quite justifiable, even though the *Romanstudien* were written after the prose works, for they are as much a critique of his own technical shortcomings as they are an analysis of the techniques of others.

Since from the *Romanstudien* as well as from the diaries and letters of Ludwig it is clear that one of his most important convictions as an artist was the idea that literature should offer not only an authentic experience, but also a certain measure of practical wisdom, I also observed his attempts to cope with the problem of realizing his dual aim of truth to reality and ideal content. As I did so a larger vista opened up, for it proved to be most enlightening in terms of the over-all development of German literature during the first half of the nineteenth century to see how one of the foremost representatives of that generation attempted to steer the difficult middle course, which so many of his contemporaries were attempting to follow, between real and ideal, and to chart his progress toward an individual solution of the dilemma which he and his generation faced together: that of creating out of the essentially unheroic reality of their own times works of art which would be both a true reflection of that reality and a value experience capable of uplifting the reader and of enriching him spiritually by broadening and deepening his human understanding.

The kind of realism which Ludwig describes as "poetischer Realismus" may be considered a natural development within the German national literary tradition insofar as it was a focusing of tendencies already present in the works of Lessing, Herder, and the classical and romantic writers. Even in its beginnings, however, it was also, as Julian Schmidt has pointed out, a break with that tradition.[4] Writing as one for whom this type of writing was contemporary literature, Schmidt declares that it must be symptomatic of a break in a nation's literary tradition when one finds it necessary, as he did in writing about the literature of his own day, to distinguish between "idealists" and "realists." For, since all literature is an idealized representation of experienced reality, and since all literature expresses its ideals in terms of the figures, situations, and events of reality, one should be able, he argues, to use the two terms almost synonymously when talking about literary art. He finds that he is easily able to do so when discussing the literature of classical antiquity and concludes that the reason must be the harmonious rapport which still existed then between man and nature. This close rapport, as he reasons it, made for a perfect correspondence between art and reality, in the sense that it enabled artists to find readily in the reality around them the correlatives necessary for the creation of their poetic works. In his own age such a harmonious rapport between subject and object is no longer possible, he finds, because of the rapidly changing real situation; and he explains largely in terms of this cultural-historical difference the emergence during the nineteenth century of the new type of writer who has become the dominant type of artist-personality in his day, and whom he calls a "one-sided idealist" or "realist."[5]

The dilemma of these writers, in Schmidt's view, was their inability to find any longer in the reality of their own experience the events, figures, and images, and the thoughts, feelings, and deeds which they required in order to create artistic works of enduring beauty and value like those of the great artists of the past. Schmidt contributes here a most valuable insight into the problem of "poetic realism," for one of the greatest challenges which these writers faced was indeed that of finding in reality situations suitable for expressing the sort of value experience which they felt literature should communicate.

Ever since Julian Schmidt first added the term *Realismus* to the terminology of literary criticism in Germany a century ago[6] German critics have been wrestling with the question: what is it that makes a "realistic" work "realistic"? The problem has become only the more complex as a result of the fact that the so-called "age of realism" extends from 1830 to 1890.[7] Even after a century, however, no satisfactory answer has been found, and the term still remains a vague concept, in the sense that it is neither adequate for characterizing the movement of literary realism as a whole in any satisfactory way or for discussing the special classes and categories of phenomena within that period.

One of the most important recent attempts to clarify the term somewhat is Richard Brinkmann's provocative study, *Wirklichkeit und Illusion. Studien über Gehalt und Grenzen des Begriffs Realismus für die erzählende Dichtung des neunzehnten Jahrhunderts* (Tübingen: Niemeyer 1957). If earlier critics have failed to shed much light on the problem of realism, Brinkmann holds, it is because they have made the mistake of considering literature almost exclusively from the point of view of its empirical content only. The purpose of his study is both to point out the inadequacies of such an approach and to suggest a new one which he believes will open the way to a far better understanding of the real implications of the movement. The first part of his study is an extended discussion of the term "realism" in which he attempts to show how *"erworbene Fracht an Bedeutungsgehalt"* has accumulated over the years. German critics, he observes, have approached the problem of realism in two essentially different ways hitherto. The majority, he finds, have followed the example of Julian Schmidt who, all but ignoring formal and aesthetic considerations, evaluated the works of the realists almost exclusively in terms of their empirical content alone. He includes in this group Adolf Stern, Richard M. Meyer, Oskar Walzel, Hans Kindermann, Max Nussberg and several others. As the extreme example of this approach he cites the studies of Georg Lukács, even going so far as to assert that the writings of the realists seem to have interested Lukács only insofar as they can be shown to mark stages on the way toward the proletarian revolution![8] He is more sympathetic toward the critics who have used the second type of approach: that of beginning with the work of art itself and considering it, apart from its empirical content, as a separate world of experience created by the artist. The most famous example of this approach, which was initiated by Clemens Lugowski in his study, *Form der Individualitäten im Roman* (Berlin, 1932), is Erich Auerbach's *Mimesis* (Bern, 1946). Brinkmann approves of Auerbach's manner of approaching the problem of represented reality in literary art, but he also takes him to task somewhat for his surprisingly free use of the term "realism" and its derivatives in his chapter on *Germinie Lacerteux*. *Mimesis* is, of course, obviously about literary realism, since its main aim is to trace from antiquity to the present the development of attitudes toward reality and of techniques for representing reality in literary art. In the chapter on Virginia Woolf, however, Auerbach tells us quite specifically (488-489) that we should not consider the book as being in any sense a history of realism, since to have undertaken such a task would have involved, as he explains, not only complex problems of chronology, but also the difficult task of defining the term "realism" itself, whose elusiveness he apparently also felt. When we read this passage we are all the more astonished at the manner in which he uses the term and its derivatives in the chapter on *Germinie Lacerteux*, where they have essentially the same meaning which Julian Schmidt and his followers assigned to them. It is only because he uses the terms in this very restricted sense that he can assert as flatly as he does in this chapter (459) that there was no literary realism in Germany before the appearance of Thomas Mann's *Buddenbrooks* in 1901!

In pursuit of his own idea, that we can clear up the confusion surrounding the term "realism" only by examining in some detail the structural form of various representative works from the period between 1830 to 1890, Brinkmann offers interpretations of Grillparzer's *Der arme Spielmann*, Otto Ludwig's *Zwischen Himmel und Erde*, and Eduard von Keyserling's *Beate und Mareile*. His method, unlike Auerbach's, is to discuss these works in their entirety and in the greatest possible detail, stressing particularly the opening pages, since these reveal, even at the outset, the kind of structural problems which the writer must contend with throughout the work. His analyses are actually answers to two basic questions which he raises in regard to each of these works: 1) of what nature must the reality of a work of art be in order to make us think of it as "realistic"? and 2) must this reality be objectively represented as something independent of the recording subject and uncolored by his ideas and attitudes? In answering these questions Brinkmann not only investigates thoroughly the structural organization of the works in question; he also has much to say about the profound changes which occurred in the artist's relationship to reality as the century advanced.

As his "norm" Brinkmann has chosen Goethe's *Wahlverwandtschaften*, which he considers as a truly objective work, both in the sense that its style-level is always the same, and in the sense that everything individual in it, all subjective self-willing on the part of the characters, is integrated in an orderly way into a higher, all-encompassing moral framework which is the ideal frame of reference within which the work is conceived. In Grillparzer's story, Brinkmann finds, we still sense as we do in Goethe's novel the glimmering of a higher moral framework. In Ludwig's tale, on the other hand, the world, he feels, has become simply "Umwelt," the environment as defined by sociology and by the natural sciences; the ideal reality, which for Goethe had been the ultimate reality and which Grillparzer had still shown as the inner possession of his hero, exists in *Zwischen Himmel und Erde* only as goodness and kindness in an individual psychological sense. In Keyserling's work, he concludes, even the postulate of an ideal nexus has vanished; for, since reality exists there only as something experienced by the individual, as he points out, moral values perforce become subjectified in corresponding degree.

Fully as interesting as Brinkmann's approach and his method is his interpretation of the works of Grillparzer, Ludwig, and Keyserling as expressions of the existential experience of individual human beings. By pointing out this about them he enables us to see them not only as examples of the new techniques for representing reality which were devised by the realists, but also as connecting links in the line of development which culminated in the psychological realism of our own age.

Although Brinkmann is unquestionably justified in criticizing many of the German critics who have written on realism for emphasizing empirical content over formal considerations, he goes too far, as some of his German colleagues have pointed out, in insisting that the only way to determine what is realistic about a literary work is to analyze its structure.[9] In my own study I have followed a middle course, as it were, considering the stories of Ludwig both as formal structures and as reflections of the *Zeitgeist*, to the extent that they are such. My method is not unlike that recently proposed by Fritz Martini.[10] Convinced as he is that we can arrive at an understanding of the nature, history, and function of poetic works only by studying them closely as structures of experience, Martini has suggested as an approach to the problem of realism a method which would preserve the best features of a rational critical approach such as Lukács's, but without being so one-sided: "Vielmehr muss sich der von Lukács mit hoher Differenzierung durchgeführten Reduktion auf eine durchwaltende Grundperspektive, die ihre Axiome aus dem politisch-gesellschaftlichen Bereich bezieht und über die Dichtung hinaus auf ihn hinzielt, sie also zu ihm in ein, wenn auch komplexes, Abhängigkeits-Verhältnis kausaler und funktionaler Art bringt, eine Methode entgegensetzen, die mit ähnlicher konkreter Rationalität das dichterische Werk als sein Fragenzentrum betrachtet und aus seiner immanenten Analyse die ihm eigene Geschichtlichkeit und seine Beziehung zum Geschichtsprozess bis in die Einzelvervästelungen von Thematik und Form begreift." I have approached the narrative works of Ludwig in this way, considering each as "ein ästhetisch in sich bestimmtes und zugleich geschichtlich gewordenes Gebilde," as Martini suggests.

Had I wished a motto for my study I could scarcely have found a better one than Robert Penn Warren's remarks on the relationship between structure and meaning in poetic art on the occasion of his receiving the National Book Award for the year 1957. His remarks[11] refer specifically to poetry, to be sure, but they apply equally well to all literary forms. He begins by saying that it is natural to think of a poem as a structure of meanings, since all of the elements which enter into its making – words, images, events, ideas, even rhyme and meter – have meaning. It is nevertheless always something more than this, he continues, in the sense that it is not only a structure of meanings, but also a structure with meaning. This meaning, he points out, is one which cannot be equated with any or all of the meanings which went into the making of the structure; and he accordingly suggests that we consider in a poem both the "structure of meanings" and the "meaning of structure." If we read a poem in this way, he concludes, it will become for us "a structure of experience which can give us the experience of a structure." I have discussed Ludwig's fictional writings in this way, both as structures of experience and as attempts to impart the experience of a structure.

CHAPTER I

# THE DECISION TO BECOME A WRITER
## DAS HAUSGESINDE

Otto Ludwig's ambition as a young man was to become a composer, and from his twentieth year on he spent several hours each day poring over scores (mainly operas), studying theory and counterpoint (unfortunately from sadly outdated handbooks), composing operas, *Lieder*, and orchestral works, and playing and analyzing his compositions with a small group of intimate friends.[1] In April 1837 he won local recognition when one of his operas, *Die Geschwister*, was performed twice under his direction in Eisfeld, and the warm reception accorded his work greatly encouraged him. He realized, however, that he still had much to learn about composition and was now more anxious than ever to study with someone who could give him the expert guidance he required. His Uncle Otto, who realized how gifted his nephew was and who could easily have provided the necessary money, hesitated to offer his help because as yet no recognition had come from outside; and thus it seemed for a time as though Ludwig would never be able to realize his wish. Then, early in 1839, he had the idea of sending the manuscript of his new operetta, *Die Köhlerin*, to the Director of Music at the Court of Meiningen. An invitation to Meiningen followed shortly, and when Ludwig returned to Eisfeld he was the proud holder of a ducal stipend. This scholarship made it possible for him to begin work that fall with Felix Mendelssohn in Leipzig.

Although Leipzig still had a number of writers in residence, including a few members of the group known as *Junges Deutschland*,[2] it no longer had as a literary center the brilliance which had won it such renown a century earlier. As a musical center, however, it was rapidly acquiring prominence. Robert Schumann, Albert Lortzing, and Felix Mendelssohn were all living there, and during the season one gala event followed the other. One of the most sparkling occasions of the 1840's was Mendelssohn's lavish reception for Franz Liszt in the *Gewandhaus*.

Ludwig, who had never been in a large city before, found Leipzig bewildering, and his beginnings there were most inauspicious. En route a trunk containing his compositions had somehow gone astray, and since Mendelssohn naturally wanted to see his earlier work before planning a course of study for him, the lost trunk occasioned several weeks' delay. The trunk finally turned up, but when Mendelssohn saw Ludwig's compositions his recommendation was to stop composing altogether for a while and concentrate on theory. He also advised him to hear as much live music as possible. This was, of course, sound advice. The difficulty was that Ludwig's budget would not stand the additional expense of opera and concert tickets. As if this were not enough, a painful swelling and stiffening in Ludwig's hands forced him to give up practicing the piano and improvising during the winter of 1839-40. He also found it increasingly difficult to attend concerts, for whenever he did go he suffered chills. He persisted for a while, even at the risk of incurring these unpleasant symptoms, but as the winter progressed he began to experience discomfort from listening to music, which seemed mixed with whistling sounds.[3] During this period of lowered vitality and enforced inactivity he turned once again to writing poetry.[4]

Early in 1840 he chanced to see in an issue of one of the popular periodicals of the day, *Die Eilpost für Moden*, a notice soliciting contributions in fiction, and the idea occurred to him that he might perhaps be able to supplement his slender income by writing and selling a story. He set to work at once, writing almost without interruption, and in an incredibly short time had finished his manuscript which he sent off with all possible haste. The story came back with a polite letter of rejection, but Ludwig, undaunted, revised and resubmitted it. Although the editor was still unenthusiastic, he forwarded the manuscript to another periodical, *Der Komet*, which, to Ludwig's delight, accepted it. The first installment appeared on April 19, 1840.[5]

As the first work of an inexperienced writer *Das Hausgesinde* of course has many flaws. Its subtitle is quite appropriate: it is really nothing more than a *Laune*. Around the basic situation, the rivalry of the simple-minded hero and the philandering count for the love of the heroine, Röschen, Ludwig builds a harmless comedy of intrigue whose action is impelled forward not by a clash of character on character, but by the author's arbitrary manipulation of circumstances. The framework of incidents is both conventional and needlessly circumstantial. The plot centers not around *one*, but around *three* boxes, and Ludwig's main concern seems to be to manipulate these three objects in such a way as to keep both the characters and the reader in a state of hopeless confusion until the very end, when their contents are finally revealed. The characters are as conventional as the plot. All are so much like puppets that we have difficulty in feeling them as real human beings and accordingly do not care what happens to them.

In this first effort we naturally sense many influences. The amorous count, the plot of the lovers to thwart him, and the jealous countess at once remind us of the basic situation in Ludwig's favorite opera, *Le Nozze di Figaro*, but his characters are not nearly so sensitively and subtly drawn. His count has none of Almaviva's charm, and his countess completely lacks the dignity and grace of her Mozartian counterpart. The hero would be likeable enough, were it not for his eternal bungling and his stupidity; but the heroine is hopelessly dull in her faithfulness.

There are also echoes of Tieck, E. T. A. Hoffmann, and the romantic *Kunstmärchen* in *Das Hausgesinde*. The manner in which Ludwig suddenly introduces the element of the wondrous in the scenes in which the dwarf Hanspeter appears at first strikes us as quite similar to Hoffmann's use of the wondrous in his *Wirklichkeitsmärchen*. A closer look at Ludwig's story soon makes it clear, however, that what at first seemed affinities are in reality only superficial resemblances, for the element of the wondrous serves quite a different function in Hoffmann's tales.[5]

In most of the *Wirklichkeitsmärchen* the pattern is the same: a character, usually the hero, is suddenly catapulted from the everyday world into another sphere where wondrous things happen, and to which he is thenceforth able to return again and again, experiencing there each time all manner of adventures.[6] Although these may seem fantastic, both to the character and to the reader, they prove nevertheless to be real enough, for they most often lead to some kind of a spiritual transformation. The experience of the wondrous is thus not an escape from reality. Nor does it give licence to shirk the fundamental human obligation to lead a purposeful life. Its end-result, in most cases, is to provide new insights which make possible a superior adjustment to reality.[7]

How does this compare to what we find in *Das Hausgesinde*? The element of the wondrous enters when the dwarf Hanspeter (who bears a striking resemblance to Hoffmann's Klein Zaches!) suddenly appears while Andres, the hero, is lying in wait for the count's valet who has been commissioned by the count to carry a gift and a message to Röschen. The conversation between Andres and the dwarf has all the qualities of a dream-experience and recalls interestingly the first important conversation between Peregrinus and his flea-mentor in Hoffmann's delightful tale, *Meister Floh*.[8] In the course of this conversation a question of Andres' prompts the strange little fellow to air his views on the difference between dreams and reality. The former, half tipsy from having drunk too much at the public festival in honor of the count's birthday, asks how he can be certain that his conversation with his tiny interlocutor is not a dream. To this query Hanspeter replies with a rhetorical question, "Was ist denn wahr?" and proceeds to answer it himself. "Was wir glauben", he declares, "ist wahr. Es gibt kein Spiel, oder alles ist Spiel. Viele nennen das wahr, was sie mit den Händen greifen, und das ist gerade die handgreiflichste Lüge. Was wir glauben und inwendig sind, davon haben wir die nächste unmittelbare Kunde (W, I, 14)." Both the circumstances under which these remarks are made and the remarks themselves remind us of similar sequences in Hoffmann's tales. Here the similarity ends, however, for the only purpose of the Hanspeter sequence, as it turns out, is to introduce into the action one of the three boxes which play such an important part in the *denouement*. The element of the wondrous serves thus not to add an interesting new dimension, as in the tales of Hoffmann, but the trivial purpose of adding complications to an already extremely confusing plot. For this reason the Hanspeter sequences might be cited as the most glaring example in the story of Ludwig's inability at this point in his development to understand the function of some of the techniques and devices which he had so freely borrowed.

Considered as a whole *Das Hausgesinde* seems rather like a patchwork quilt without a distinct pattern. The lack of coherence stems in part, to be sure, from the fact that in order to save time Ludwig incorporated into his story elements from earlier works.[9] But it can also be explained in terms of Ludwig's lack of knowledge of the fine points of the narrative writer's craft. The only real evidence of his later skill is the brief sequence near the beginning in which he describes the village festival in honor of the count's birthday (*W*, I, 5-6). The scene recalls Breughel's portrayals of village life. Enormous tables groan under the weight of immense quantities of food; vast casks filled with cider repose in the cool shade of the bushes; and the villagers, in gay holiday attire, throng the streets. Ludwig focuses attention first on the elderly matrons, whose stiffly starched dresses, which sway from side to side as they walk, give them the appearance of "bells moving on their clappers." Then with a few rapid strokes of his pen he sketches the merry group of peasant boys and girls in their Sunday finery. By citing only five details he succeeds in imparting a vivid impression of the sun-tanned peasant lads with their sturdy legs and freely swinging arms, whose easy, graceful movements betray long practice in cracking a whip; and with three more he suggests the fresh beauty of the girls: "Da wehten die kurzen Röckchen um die gedrängte Form der kecken Dirnen, die bunten Bänder um die bräunlichen Heckenrosen der vollen Gesichter." With great deftness he then summarizes the busy scene by means of a series of impersonal expressions which suggest the many different activities which are going on simultaneously as the villagers make the most of this rare festive occasion:

> Da ward gezupft und geneckt, die Augen verdeckt, der Verdecker erraten. Da flogen Winke und Blicke, da klang Gesang und Gelächter... Da versteckte sich die Verschämtheit geheim sich wähnender Neigung vor den nicht schonenden Anspielungen hinter verlegenem Gekicher und scheinbar unbefangenem Eingehen auf den Scherz. Da lächelte sich Einfalt und harmlose Liebe aus vollen freundlichen Gesichtern zu, da stierte die Gedankenlosigkeit ins Blaue, da zog der Neid die Mundwinkel, da haftete sich der grimmig versteckte Blick der Eifersucht an jeden Zug seines Gegenstandes, da wiegte sich die Selbstgefälligkeit auf Schuh- und Stiefelspitzen, da spreizte sich der plumpe Geldstolz, da zierte sich die Gefallsucht, da schnellten die Pfeile von den Augenbrauen der ländlichen Koketten. Wer niemand anderm gefiel, der gefiel doch sich, wer kein Publikum fand, belachte seine Spässe selbst.

What makes this scene seem authentic is that it reflects Ludwig's own experience, for it is a picture of the kind of village celebrations which he had often witnessed in his native Thuringia. Hence his sureness of touch. In its truth to reality, and also in its delightful humor it foreshadows his later masterpieces about provincial life, *Die Heiteretei* and *Aus dem Regen in die Traufe*. It is, however, the only bright spot in an otherwise rather insipid story which disappoints us on the whole as a work weak in formal organization, obscure and confusing in plot, and totally lacking in any kind of profundity - in short, as a vision of reality which fails to come to life.

The illness which had afflicted Ludwig during the winter of 1839-40 had undermined his morale to the point where he had begun to doubt whether he could ever succeed as a composer. Along with these doubts, however, there had also grown a new conviction: that his real forte as an artist was the creation of poetic forms.[10] Both his doubts and his new conviction caused him to long for a quiet existence, perhaps as a music teacher in a small town like Eisfeld, where he would have peace of mind and the freedom to work as he wished at his various literary and musical projects.[11] This longing, coupled with his dread of another winter in Leipzig, made him immediately receptive to Mendelssohn's suggestion that he could study the technical aspects of composition as profitably in Eisfeld as in Leipzig, and by the end of October he had finished his preparations to leave. He arrived home at the end of November full of enthusiasm and eager to work.

CHAPTER II

# A PARODY
## DIE EMANZIPATION DER DOMESTIKEN

Ludwig completed the first draft of his second story sometime in mid-October of 1840 shortly before leaving Leipzig for Eisfeld, and by the end of the year he was putting the finishing touches to the final version. Since he needed money, as usual, he was, of course, anxious to sell his manuscript as soon as possible, but another idea had also suggested itself. Modest though he was about his own work he believed the story not altogether without merit, and since he had as yet done nothing as a composer to justify the high expectations of the Duke of Meiningen, the thought had occurred to him that his royal patron might be willing to extend his stipend on the strength of his ability as a writer. The Duke had the manuscript read by his Court Librarian, Ludwig Bechstein, who enjoyed a modest reputation as a writer, and the verdict was quite favorable. Bechstein's positive comments convinced the Duke that Ludwig's scholarship should be renewed. When the manuscript was returned Ludwig sent it off to Heinrich Laube, who was then the editor of *Die Zeitung für die elegante Welt*, and it was accepted in spite of its satirical diatribes against "Young Germany." It was printed in two installments in June and July of 1843.

Although a number of characters appear in the three actions which occur in *Die Emanzipation der Domestiken* our attention is finally focused on two, the heroine, Florentine, and the chief steward of the castle who is responsible for the "emancipation" of the servants announced in the title. Florentine's independence of spirit is admirable, without doubt, and we also follow with at least mild interest the course of her development from a romantic girl into a mature woman who finds in her love for her unknown benefactor the answer to her restless seeking. Far more original as a character, however, and certainly much more amusing, is the "emancipator" of the servants. This strange fellow, who recalls some of Jean Paul's eccentrics, has literally devoured the works of Gutzkow, Mundt, Laube, George Sand, and other "emancipatory" writers of the day, and when we first meet him he, too, is about to proclaim a great emancipatory idea. It is based on his discovery, which he considers quite revolutionary, that human beings possess not one, but two intellectual bases for their actions, their "right reason" and their "left reason."[1] By "right reason" he means a peculiar combination of intellect and intuition which enables people to act in the right way automatically without undue reflection. He thinks of "left reason," on the other hand, as the tendency of most people to weigh carefully all aspects of a situation before acting, a tendency which he feels leads most often to wrong actions or to no action at all. Ironically enough, events bear out the wisdom of what he proclaims here, for by "emancipating" himself from his servile attitude and following his "right reason," which prompts him to disobey an order of his mistress, he saves the castle from the attacking robbers and so becomes the real hero of the story!

One unfamiliar with Ludwig's other writings might conclude from his gentle lampooning of *Junges Deutschland* through the figure of the *Haushofmeister* that he was not seriously concerned over the activities of the *Jungdeutschen*. In reality, however, he strongly opposed them. Even as a young writer he held that literature should not only entertain but also exert a wholesome moral influence. It was accordingly a basic tenet of his that literature should reflect a definite moral point of view. In many writers of his day he missed this. Far too many, he felt, were willing to follow the easy way to success by titillating jaded appetites or by appealing to sentiment through falsely idealizing pictures of reality; and among the worst offenders, in his opinion, were the *Jungdeutschen* whom he found guilty both of deceiving their readers, by offering them chimeras instead of realities, and of undermining their sense of values by catering to their taste for the sensational. Irresponsible writers of this sort, the critics who praise them, and the men who publish their works were in large measure responsible, he felt, for the low ebb of contemporary literary and cultural life and for the lack of moral concern which he found everywhere.[2] In Ludwig's opinion the most urgent problems facing the age were neither the emancipation of the feminine sex, to which the *Jungdeutschen* devoted so much attention, nor the political and social questions which had preoccupied such writers as Saint-Simon and François Fourier, but moral and ethical problems. No society could be said to exist on a solid foundation, he believed, until it had found solutions for such basic problems as, for example, the tendency to judge other human beings by such shallow standards as wealth and social position rather than in terms of their moral qualities, which Ludwig considered the only valid measure of an individual. He took issue with all of the liberal social reformers of his day because of their seeming lack of concern with such problems.[3]

Ludwig's sharp criticisms of *Junges Deutschland* might well lead one to assume that he took issue with the *Jungdeutschen* on aesthetic grounds as well. A comparison of their views reveals, however, many interesting affinities. Like Ludwig, the *Jungdeutschen* also assigned to literature the highest place among the arts, just as their predecessors, the writers of the classical and romantic generations had done. Even the main point on which they differed from their predecessors was one with which Ludwig was in full agreement, for he, too, held that for those of his own day an aesthetic education was far from adequate. The most fundamental resemblances between Ludwig and the *Jungdeutschen*, however, are to be found in their views relating to the work of art as a revelation of the *Wahrheit* which inheres in *Wirklichkeit*.

Most of the *Jungdeutschen*, as is well known, were students of Hegel, and he, of course, influenced profoundly both their world-outlook and their aesthetic views.[4] From his lectures and writings they learned to look at the universe in a new way and acquired a new conception of the phenomenon of being, for he taught them to see the phenomenal world as animated and informed by an all-pervading spirit which is immanent in all the forms of reality, a spirit whose essential nature is endless change and development, and whose purpose is self-revelation and self-realization through the multiplicity of real forms which we perceive about us.[5] All life was in Hegel's eyes, one might say, the living expression of an *Idea* whose essential nature, or whose essential truth, might be grasped by a close scrutiny of its workings as these become perceptible in actual reality, or *Wirklichkeit*. In Hegel's writings one finds numerous examples of his attempt to formulate this insight into a concept.[6]

Because Hegel's concept of absolute being was based on the idea of a perfect identity between *Wahrheit* and *Wirklichkeit* he did not hesitate to speak of his philosophy as a *Wirklichkeitsphilosophie*. To some of his students, however, particularly those who wished to respond actively to what they felt to be the challenge of the times, his system appeared too abstract and too remote from reality. Not a few objected, too, that in concentrating on the process of history he tended to lose sight of the importance of the individual. It was in the main these objections which caused the "left-wing Hegelians" to break with their teacher. Even though they disagreed with him, however, they continued to venerate him, and all of them, too, continued to employ his dialectical method in working out their own philosophical and aesthetic problems.[7]

The aesthetic program of the *Jungdeutschen* reflects both their close identification with their own age and their desire to serve it in some positive way through their art. In his preface to his *Aesthetische Feldzüge* Ludolf Wienbarg exhorts all of the young writers of his day to turn to the world about them for the substance of their art.[8] When he insists that literary art should be based on actual reality, however, he does not mean that a literary work should be a mirror image of reality. For he shared Hegel's view that an artist should attempt to make his work a fusion of *Wirklichkeit* and *Wahrheit*. Theodor Mundt is saying essentially the same thing when he describes the purpose of art as that of representing "...die objektive Wirklichkeit des wissenden und schaffenden Geistes auf ihrem rein ideellen Gebiete..."[9] Gutzkow, as we noted earlier, also considered as the highest kind of artistic expression a work which offers the reader both of these experiences simultaneously. He expresses this idea in verse in his *Neue Kunstregeln*: "Zweierlei drängt jetzt den Dichter: der Kunst die Reize der Neuheit, / Jene Wahrheit zu leih'n, die den Ideen entquillt, / Oder, solang die Idee mit der Welt, mit sich selbst noch streitet, / Wenigstens, was sie schon hat, alte Bewährung, Natur / Ewig zu sichern..."[10]

Realism never became for the *Jungdeutschen* as it did for the naturalists a value *per se*. One might indeed say that it never became more than a facet of their art. What they strove to achieve was an art equal to the finest works of the classicists and romanticists in "ideal content," but which would at the same time be close to actual reality. Gutzkow, who was so often the spokesman of the *Jungdeutschen* in aesthetic matters, states the case very succinctly when he proclaims that the only idealism worth striving for in art is one which is rooted in actuality and which reveals itself "...auf Voraussetzungen der Natürlichkeit und Wirklichkeit."[11] He reaffirms this when he defines the new type of novel which he and his contemporaries were attempting to create as a bulwark against the tendentiousness, the materialistic values, and the exaggerated, daguerreotype kind of realism which he deplored so greatly in the literature of his times, both at home and abroad.[12]

One might say, in summary, that the aesthetic ideal of the *Jungdeutschen* was "realized ideality" rather than "idealized reality," which all condemned as unworthy. In literary works they found this quality less often than in painting. The painters in whose works they found it to a very high degree were Raphael, Dürer, and two of the Nazarenes, Schnorr von Carolsfeld and Peter Cornelius. To describe the fusion of real and ideal which he found in the works of such painters Ruge used the term "noble naturalism" (*edler Naturalismus*), and he did not hesitate to proclaim this quality the highest toward which an artist can aspire. Ruge's definition of "noble naturalism" is a beautifully succinct statement of the aesthetic ideal of all of the *Jungdeutschen*: "Dieser edle Naturalismus wäre allerdings der wahre Idealismus; denn er ist das Sehen durch die natürlichen Erscheinungen vermittelst derselben, die eben dadurch edel werden, dass sie den Geist zeigen."[13]

While the *Jungdeutschen* were generally in agreement, at least in principle, with the view of most of the classical and romantic writers, that a work of art should possess some kind of universal significance, they did not share their predecessors' ideas on the importance of form. As writers dedicated to the active service of their age through their art they considered content far more important than form.[14] Since their purpose was to provide through their writings a direct impetus toward change, and since most of them felt that they could best realize this activistic aim by writing in a striking and energetic manner, they tended to stress forcefulness over beauty and perfection of form. They had no serious pretensions to becoming classical writers, and most of them admitted quite frankly their aesthetic shortcomings.[15]

Ludwig believed as the *Jungdeutschen* did that the writer should seek the raw materials of his art in the world around him. Reality, or *Wirklichkeit*, thus meant for him too the world of feelings, passsions, and effects rather than the world of abstract thoughts and concepts. He also shared their view that the creative artist is a superiorly endowed individual who is able both to perceive higher meanings behind apparent reality and to impart these meanings to others through the symbols of his art, and he sought, as they did, to reveal these higher meanings. While seeking in his art the same ideal fusion of *Wirklichkeit* and *Wahrheit* as the *Jungdeutschen* did, however, his ideas as to how it might best be realized differed strikingly from theirs.[16] For he was convinced that the fusion of the two could be attained only in the most carefully structured works of art. Unlike the *Jungdeutschen*, Ludwig always placed great stress on the importance of form in art. The kind of form which he strove to achieve was not the kind which Coleridge refers to as "mechanic,"[17] but rather an inner, organic type of form which he attempted to impart to his works by fitting together their structural elements and their meanings in such a way as to make them seem independently existing microcosms containing within themselves, just as the real world does, all of their own conditions and consequences. Poetic worlds so constructed are, he believed, just as real as the real world, even though they are products of an artist's imagination.[18]. While they are as real as the real world, however, they also differ from it in two essential ways. In the first place, unlike nature, which is essentially "open" in the sense that it has no perceptible boundaries or limits, the world of the work of art is "closed," since art is finite. In the second place, created as it is out of selected aspects of the artist's experience and consciously organized by him, it perforce acquires a transparency which actual reality lacks. In the artist's world not only the over-all structural pattern, but also the literal and symbolic meanings stand out more clearly than in the everyday world.[19]

*Die Emanzipation der Domestiken* unfortunately fell far short of becoming an ideal fusion of *Wirklichkeit* and *Wahrheit*. With all due respect to Bechstein, we cannot help feeling that the story suffers from the worst faults which we observed in *Das Hausgesinde*. Many of the flaws which we note are attributable to the fact that in writing the story Ludwig borrowed somewhat too freely from his various sources.[20] The motive of the disappearing village, which, since it has no apparent function in the story, seems to have been a random borrowing, comes from folk-lore; and there are numerous parallels in the works of Schiller, Vulpius, Kleist, Grillparzer, Hauff, and other less well known writers for the action involving the robbers. The strange elective affinity which draws the hero and heroine together reminds us dimly of Goethe's *Wahlverwandtschaften*; and the *Haushofmeister's* mock chivalry in defending the castle against the attacking robbers recalls sequences in *Don Quixote* which Ludwig had read in German translation in 1840. Throughout the work we also feel the aura of Gothic romance and of the historical novels which Scott and his German imitators had made popular in Germany. An even more obvious influence, of course, is that of Tieck. We think of such works as *Das Zauberschloss, Die Wundersüchtige, Der Mondsüchtige, Eigensinn und Laune* (which contains the motive of "left" and "right" reason), *Aufruhr in den Cevennen*, and others.

The most serious defect of *Die Emanzipation der Domestiken* is its faulty structure. The architectural problem which Ludwig set for himself was that of integrating into a unified whole three essentially unrelated actions: a robber-romance revolving around a plot to attack a castle in the middle of a lonely forest; a love story which develops out of the robber-romance; and, as if that were not already enough, the emancipation of the servants announced in the title! The result is that the tale has no central emphasis. Until almost the end no one of the three actions seems more important than the others. Ludwig's intention thus remains obscure almost to the last. When we have finished the story we wonder, too, why he entitled it as he did, for, if the action involving the servants is at times amusing, it is by no means of sufficient importance to justify their figuring so prominently in the title.

We feel a similar uncertainty about the characters. After having read the opening dialogue, for example, in which Ludwig goes to great lengths to point out the differences in outlook between the romantic young baron and his more pragmatically minded young friend who is to become a police chief, we feel certain that both young men will play major roles in the subsequent action. Not so.

When the future police chief takes leave of his friend at the end of the scene he vanishes from sight to reappear only in the last pages of the tale. The baron, who is supposed to be the romantic hero of the tale, also withdraws in a sense from the action, for, as a consequence of the wound which he receives while rescuing the heroine from the robbers who have ambushed her in the forest, he lies in a semi-comatose state until the final scene!

In defense of the story, on the other hand, it must be said that the actions of the characters correspond to their temperaments and personalities to a greater degree than in *Das Hausgesinde*. It is, for example, the heroine's love of romantic adventure and her restless spirit which motivate her lonely night ride in the forest in the course of which she falls into the hands of the robbers; and it is likewise the hero's reckless daring which prompts him to try to rescue her single-handed. Since both hero and heroine are depicted as very independent natures, their psychological make-up may be said to influence the course of the action in yet another way; for it is this trait in both which makes them rebel against the marriage of convenience arranged by their parents.

The improvement which we note in Ludwig's ability to portray characters convincingly makes us feel all the more strongly his ineptness in handling the problem of bringing them into relationship with one another. Chance, we feel, plays far too prominent a role in this little world. To cite but one example among many, it is only because the hero chances to be in a particular inn at a particular time that he overhears the robbers plotting to ambush the countess's daughter in the forest. Thus even the all-important first meeting of the two romantic leads results from pure coincidence!

As in *Das Hausgesinde*, we feel in only a few passages that Ludwig is writing about what he knew from his own experience. Yet we feel even so that *Die Emanzipation der Domestiken* is somehow closer to reality. Perhaps this is because through all of the romantic trappings we feel in the story an unmistakable focusing on the everyday and the near-at-hand. For even those of high birth are depicted as ordinary human beings with ordinary human problems; and the moral at the end, that married life is best after all, is a moral for ordinary human beings. We find, in other words, a concentration on the "norm" of human experience in the tale, and this quality marks it in at least one important respect as a foreshadowing of Ludwig's later works.

To summarize, *Die Emanzipation der Domestiken* is faulty in three respects: it fails, in the first place, to satisfy us as an aesthetic experience because Ludwig did not succeed in fusing into a meaningful totality the heterogeneous elements of which he made his story. It lacks, secondly, a unifying point of view; and its third fault is its misplaced accents which cause it to fail as a parody. The style, too, is uneven. We find only isolated moments of good writing, and these only in the sequences which take place in the servants' wing of the castle. As an example I cite the concluding paragraphs describing the servants' tribute to their "emancipator":

> Da öffnete sich die Tür, und herein bewegte sich ein feierlicher Zug. Der Koch schritt voran, ihm folgten die Frauenzimmer, einen Kranz tragend, den sie in Ermangelung passenderen Grünes aus gedörrten Lorbeerblättern, Majoran, Rosmarin und anderen Kräutern des Küchenvorrats gewunden hatten. Dann kam der Kutscher, und der Küchenjunge schloss den Zug. Feierliche Stille herrschte, als sie den Hofmeister zweimal umschritten und endlich vor ihm stehen blieben. Die Frauenzimmer setzten ihm den Kranz auf, und der Kutscher räusperte sich und begann mit begeisterten, bald aber vom Weinen unterdrückten Tönen und entsprechenden Gebärden:
>
> "Grosser, Vortrefflicher, Unaussprechlicher! Nimm den Dank der Menschheit aus unsern Händen. Spiegle dich in diesen Tränen, die mir stromesweise aus den Augen laufen. Nimm unsere Versicherung, dass wir dein Werk fördern wollen, solange uns Gott das Leben schenkt. Sterben ist ein Bitteres, aber der Tod ist uns allen beschieden, er sei dusemang oder plötzlich. Brüder, Wehmut ist eine schöne Tugend. Darum lasset die Toten ruhen, denn ihnen ist wohl. Deshalb lebe unser Haushofmeister, der Erfinder der Emanzipation der Dienstboten!"
>
> "Er lebe!" hallte es von jedem Munde, und jetzt drang, die herabgebrannten Lichter beschämend, die erste Röte des Morgens durch die Fenster herein und legte ihre Glorie um die erhabene Gruppe der Umschlungenen.

We laugh here because Ludwig has expressed so effectively the discrepancy between the noble intentions of the servants and the manner in which they attempt to carry them out. Yet, could there be a more fitting tribute to the *Haushofmeister* than the wreath of dried out laurel-leaves and kitchen-herbs and the sentimentally bombastic and totally disconnected speech of the *Kutscher*? Both details are admirable inventions which attest to Ludwig's gifts as a comic writer; and the passage as a whole is an excellent example of his ability to create a scene which is alive. After reading it one can only regret that the rest of the story is so inferior to it in niveau.

CHAPTER III

## A FAIRY-TALE FROM EVERYDAY LIFE
## *DIE WAHRHAFTIGE GESCHICHTE VON DEN DREI WÜNSCHEN*

From afar Leipzig seemed a much pleasanter place to Ludwig than it had seemed while he was there, and this nostalgia and the growing certainty that he would never be able to realize his potential as an artist in the stultifying atmosphere of his native town prompted him finally to return to Leipzig in June of 1842. By this time he had made up his mind that he was going to be a writer and hence did not even look up his old teacher, but settled down at once to work in a modest room. Although he spent many hours alone, he was less withdrawn than during his first stay, and in the summer and fall of 1842 he met frequently with a group of young scholars, philosophers, and writers who gathered almost daily in Waldrich's cafe, where they spent long evenings discussing all kinds of philosophical and aesthetic problems far into the night. All of the members of this little group were interested in Ludwig's work, and some of them even found their way into the pages of his third story, *Die wahrhaftige Geschichte von den drei Wünschen*, whose cheerful tone reflects his happier adjustment to reality in those days.

From a diary entry of August 1839 we know that the idea for the new story had occurred to him several years earlier. The work, as he envisioned it then, was to be a study of German folk-ways, a *Sittengemälde*, with a contemporary German setting. In spirit, however, it was to be like the *Arabian Nights*. In writing it he planned to allow his imagination free rein and to offer his reader "...das Poetische mit dem Prosaischsten in lustiger Mischung," and to carry both "Unsichtbarkeit" and "Doppelsichtbarkeit" to the wildest extremes. Like a magician he planned to conjure up a whole imaginary world in which shoemakers, imperial counselors, potters, princes, geniuses, and fools would meet and become involved with one another in all manner of unusual adventures.[1]

Ludwig began to write toward the end of the summer of 1842 and doubtless finished the first version in February 1843. The final draft was completed late in the summer of 1843.[2] One of his new friends, the Oriental philologist Wetzstein, was so delighted with the story that he immediately offered to help him find a publisher. All efforts were futile, however, and at last it was added to the already sizable pile of manuscripts which Ludwig had brought with him from Eisfeld. It was not published until fifty years later.[3]

To make his fantastic tale of the three wishes seem as plausible as possible Ludwig presents it as a true experience related to him by an aspiring young writer. Various details suggest that this young writer, who remains anonymous throughout, is also none other than Ludwig himself, for he, too, is a musician, and in his shabby room there is also a trunkfull of unpublished manuscripts. Like the two earlier stories, *Die wahrhaftige Geschichte von den drei Wünschen* also opens with a conversation. This brief introductory dialogue sequence provides the frame for the young writer's true story of his sad love-experience, a work which he has entitled *Zu stille Liebe*. Before he begins his tale he promises his listener, our narrator, that he is about to hear adventures far more wondrous than those in the *Arabian Nights* or the tales of Hoffmann, and we soon see that he is not exaggerating a bit! As the young author tells his story the emotion of reliving his unhappy love-experience so overwhelms him that he is obliged to pause frequently in order to regain his composure. As he breaks down the first time he hands his visitor three pages from an ancient Sanskrit manuscript. These pages have come into his possession in a most remarkable manner from three different sources, and more remarkable still is the fact that together they constitute a connected narrative about the nymph Urvasi, her four daughters, and a curse placed upon these young ladies by an aged wise man named Chayava.[4] The young author assures his visitor that there is a connection between this ancient tale and the contemporary happenings recorded in his own strange narrative; but even after the latter has finished reading it (during two subsequent emotional breakdowns of the young author) he is completely in the dark (and so is the reader) as to what this connection might be. Only two details suggest at this point that the legend might have some bearing on *Zu stille Liebe*: the name Jammadagni, on the second page of the Sanskrit manuscript, which bears a resemblance to that of the father of the heroine of *Zu stille Liebe*, whose name is Jammerdegen; and the condition set forth on page three of the Sanskrit tale, that Chayava's curse can be removed only if a wealthy editor agrees to publish a work by an unknown young author and offers that same young man his daughter in marriage!

The legend of Urvasi is but the first of several interpolations. The most important of these are the tales of three *Literati* whom the author of *Zu stille Liebe* mentions having encountered one day in Waldrich's Cafe while attempting to drown his sorrows in wine. The fantastic tales of these three unhappy young men, which the young author has appended to his own sad narrative, make clear at last the significance of the title of Ludwig's story, for each revolves about a great life's wish which is momentarily realized. As the young author relates these tales, each of which is the story of a lost love, the reader gradually begins to perceive, too, the links between *Zu stille Liebe* and the legend of Urvasi. The brief autobiographical sketches with which the three *Literati* preface their tales also reveal connecting links between the lives of the *Literati* and that of the author of *Zu stille Liebe*, for each, it turns out, has been associated with some person who has crossed the path of that young man during his desperate pursuit of love and happiness. All of the wondrous happenings of *Die wahrhaftige Geschichte von den drei Wünschen* thus prove to be interconnected, and in such a way that all may be looked upon as parts of one great marvelous adventure.

Like the author of *Zu stille Liebe* and like Ludwig himself, each of the three *Literati* is of middle class origin. Their adventures also resemble in certain basic ways. Each is projected suddenly and mysteriously into a relationship with a beautiful and fabulously wealthy woman of high station, and each experiences in his romantic adventure the most perfect happiness. Even this perfect happiness proves to be not enough, however, for soon after finding it each begins to long for something beyond it; and in the case of each this longing springs from an unrealized childhood wish. In comparison with the wonderful love-experience which each has enjoyed these wishes seem most trivial. The first young man desires worldly glory; the second, material possessions; and the third craves power and authority. Thanks to the women, in whose power it lies to grant these wishes, each obtains what he desires; and to the then perfect happiness which each subsequently enjoys only one condition is attached in each case. Each forfeits his happiness by violating the oath which he has sworn to his beloved; and each, after his expulsion from his paradise, senses even more keenly than before his loneliness and isolation in the world. As a bitter reminder of lost happiness each young man carries a permanent scar, and each, in his despair, has become, amusingly enough, a writer!

With the tale of the last of the three *literati* both *Zu stille Liebe* and *Die wahrhaftige Geschichte von den drei Wünschen* come to a close. The few remaining lines return us to the frame-situation, but only long enough for the young narrator to relate briefly his ultimate failure to win Fides as his bride. Because he seems so utterly dejected we must pity him. Yet as we watch him dramatically feeling his pulse and hear him exclaim with such pathos that he must think of other things in order to go on living, we also have to smile. We wonder even, as we leave him, whether he doesn't perhaps also enjoy the experience of suffering.

Both the structural pattern of *Die wahrhaftige Geschichte von den drei Wünschen* and Ludwig's manner of representing reality in it suggest the influence of E. T. A. Hoffmann. Each of the tales of the five main narrators is, like the *Wirklichkeitsmärchen*, an account of a wondrous adventure; and each begins in a similar manner in familiar surroundings and under prosaic circumstances. We note a similarity, too, in the suddenness with which the wondrous adventures begin. Still another point of resemblance is the manner in which Ludwig's heroes experience time and space relationships while involved in their adventures; for they, too, seem to move freely backward and forward in time and to overcome with ease the spatial restrictions under which we live our lives in everyday reality. During his adventure each of Ludwig's young men acquires, moreover, the same faculty of heightened perception which Hoffmann's heroes enjoy. Interrelationships and interconnections of which they have been totally unaware suddenly become clear. They seem to become both clairvoyant and clairsentient.

The setting of *Die wahrhaftige Geschichte von den drei Wünschen* is contemporary Leipzig; yet in its pages we meet, to our endless amazement, not only contemporary figures, but also oriental gods, nymphs, and wise men from the remote mythological past. What is still more astonishing is that the characters, although they exist on different time planes historically speaking, become involved in complex interrelationships. Not a few of them possess double identities, like the characters in Hoffmann's *Wirklichkeitsmärchen*: Jammadagni, the Oriental wise man in the Sanskrit legend, is at the same time Jammerdegen, the Leipzig editor in *Zu stille Liebe*; and the latter's daughter, Fides, turns out to be one of the four daughters of Urvasi as well! The ties between past and present are made even closer through the motive of Chayava's curse, which, although pronounced at a time before the gods had become mythological figures, can be removed only by a spontaneous act of generosity by a nineteenth century Leipzig editor!

While these aspects of *Die wahrhaftige Geschichte von den drei Wünschen* remind us of Hoffmann's *Wirklichkeitsmärchen*, however, we also find differences. The most striking of these is the effect which the adventures of Ludwig's heroes have on the future course of their lives. For whereas Hoffmann's heroes often gain from their wondrous adventures a new perspective on life and reality which enables them to become better integrated personalities, Ludwig's heroes seem to gain nothing from their experiences but disappointment. The end result for each is that reality, in contrast, seems hopelessly bleak and empty. One might even say that their experiences have impaired their ability to adjust to reality, for their only visible achievement since their rude awakening to reality has been to jot down their experience in more or less anecdotal form. Otherwise they seem to spend their time wallowing in self-pity.

Through the view of reality which it reflects *Die wahrhaftige Geschichte von den drei Wünschen* offers a far better basis than either of Ludwig's earlier stories for evaluating his attitude toward romanticism as a young writer. From the accounts of all four heroes we must conclude that it was, to say the least, ambivalent. For in each account the pattern is the same: a romantic situation is painstakingly built up and then ruthlessly destroyed. We can hardly suppress the feeling that Ludwig, after having given free rein to his romantic imagination, felt compelled in each case, out of a sense of honesty, to shatter his beautiful vision.

In yet another sense the four narratives in *Die wahrhaftige Geschichte von den drei Wünschen* cause us to feel the story as a break with the romantic tradition. Inasmuch as each of the narratives involves a wish, and also because the hero, in order to gain his wish, must undergo an ordeal, we at once associate the tale as a whole with the genre which found such widespread favor among the German romantisists, the *Märchen*. The ordeals of Ludwig's heroes are even in ascending order of difficulty as they are in fairy-tales. What really strikes us about them, however, is not that each is more difficult than the preceding one, but that all of them are so absurd! The first *Literatus* must never try to see the mark which his lovely Vasanta carries on her thigh; the second must never attempt to visit his Hildeswinth on Mondays; and the third is limited to one day a week with his *Sonne des Lebens*. There is also something almost grotesque about the scars which the three *Literati* carry as souvenirs of their experiences: the first is missing an ear-lobe which Vasanta bit off in her anguish at losing him forever; the second wears a plaster on his cheek to conceal a bite-wound which is a memento of Hildeswinth's passionate farewell; and the third wears a moustache to cover the spot on his lip where *Sonne des Lebens* bit him during their farewell embrace! From Ludwig's levitous treatment of these experiences it is obvious that he intended the tales of all three *Literati* as parodies of the romantic *Kunstmärchen*; and when we recall that the young author to whom he introduces us in the frame-sequence is in all likelihood none other than himself, we see that the story as a whole is even in a sense a kind of self-parody.

If the parodying tendency of *Die wahrhaftige Geschichte von den drei Wünschen* causes us to feel it as a break with romanticism, the fact that it is parody suggests, on the other hand, that Ludwig's attitude in writing it must have been closely akin to the "ironic" attitude as defined by Friedrich Schlegel. For Schlegel, we recall, irony was both a way of looking at reality and a manner of communicating one's vision of reality to others. As an attitude toward reality it arises naturally and inevitably, he felt, out of our awareness of the paradoxical nature of our situation as finite creatures in an infinite universe which we can never hope to comprehend in its entirety.[5] The paradoxical nature of our situation is most clearly apparent in the paradoxical manner in which we experience the world in which we live; for to all of us it is a paradox in the sense that it strikes us at the same time as something both orderly and capricious. From what we know and understand about the functioning of our world we have been able to intuit a principle of causality operating in it which can be thought of as a kind of super-law controlling the universe as a whole. The intuition of this controlling causality causes us to feel the world as an ordered reality. On the other hand, the fact that we cannot apprehend this super-law, and that we are consequently unable either to predict happenings or to understand fully the things that have happened, makes the world seem at the same time highly unpredictable. Only a few gifted individuals – seers, prophets, philosophers, poets – have from time to time gained momentary insight into the mystery of the higher workings of the universe, but because of the limited powers of all human beings to communicate, their expression of what they have perceived or intuited always falls short of ultimate reality.[6]

In the creative artist the ironic attitude arises, Schlegel felt, both out of an awareness of the fundamentally unbridgeable chasm between the real and the ideal and out of a realization, in the presence of the work at hand, of the eternal disparity between ideal visions and the ability to express these adequately in artistic form. The kind of perspective gained through this dual awareness is such, he believed, as to enable the ironic artist to become detached to the point of being able to see objectively not only the aspect or aspects of real experience from which he draws the raw materials of his art, but also the work itself as he shapes it out of his raw materials.[7]

Inasmuch as the ironic attitude arises thus out of an awareness of the paradoxical nature of reality and of our experience of reality, the form best suited to express it, in Schlegel's view, is the paradox. The truly ironic work is always paradoxical, he maintained, in the sense that it is the conscious imposition of form, that is of unity, symmetry, and harmony, on the heterogeneous, disorganized, and hence essentially formless elements of the artist's original experience. In the greatest poetic ironic works what appears to be complete guilelessness and spontaneity is thus in reality the most complete artifice, and the pattern of the whole, though seemingly casually made, is in reality one whose every detail has been thoughtfully planned, and in which, as a result, even the most trivial details are related in an integral way to the design of the whole.[8]

Because of its loose structure *Die wahrhaftige Geschichte von den drei Wünschen* falls short of the requirements for the perfect ironic work. Ludwig's main aim, it would seem, is to dazzle us with the richness of his imagination. His ability to invent characters and episodes is, indeed, quite impressive. The story's sixty-five pages are crammed full of episodes, and we meet in them a host of characters, many of whom are quite distinctive. Far from being dazzled by Ludwig's virtuosity, however, we find ourselves instead becoming increasingly more impatient with him for confusing us as he does. For we meet so many different personalities and find the plot so involved that we must keep constantly turning back in order to keep things sorted out. Not until we have read well over a third of the story do we begin to have an inkling of how its various elements fit together. One feels that Ludwig wrote it without any real perspective of the work as a whole. Some episodes have no apparent function. Herr Flötenspiel's anecdote about the Seven Years' War, which has no visible connection with anything else, is an example in point. One is left with the impression that Ludwig was so enchanted by each new character and situation which he imagined that he simply developed each for its own sake without considering its relationship to the overall design and intention of his work.

Because *Die wahrhaftige Geschichte von den drei Wünschen* is so fantastic we almost forget, in reading it, that it was also supposed to be *wahrhaftig*. Ludwig sought in various ways to make it seem so: its setting is contemporary Leipzig; rational explanations are suggested for many of its fantastic happenings; and it is narrated by someone whom we actually see before us. With the exception of a few sequences, however, episodes such as Herr Heidermann's birthday party or the third *Literat's* account of his experiences as a child-beggar in the employ of Dame Müller, the tale seems anything but *wahrhaftig*. Considered as a whole it seems much more a product of pure fancy than of realistic observation.

What causes us to feel it as weak, however, is not so much its failure to come to life as its lack of integration, and hence its lack of artistic intensity. Yet even with its formal defects it is not altogether without charm, and here and there we even find bits which are quite good. One example among several is the opening paragraph in the story of the first *Literat* (*W*, I, 132):

> "In meinem siebenzehnten Jahre," begann der erste Literat seine Geschichte, "in meinem siebenzehnten Jahre war ich Laufbursche bei dem Schuhmachermeister Fintlein in der kleinen Fleischergasse. Ich fühlte auf das lebendigste in mir, dass ich zu andern Dingen bestimmt sei als zum Wasserholen, Stiefelwichsen und was damals noch sonst meines Amtes war. Da ich nun dies alles mit Widerwillen trieb, so ist es kein Wunder, dass es oft nicht zu meinem Lobe ausfiel und ich böser Worte genug vernehmen musste, was meinen Wider-

willen nur wieder verstärkte. Das einzige, was in jenen Tagen trauriger Knechtschaft mich erhielt, war ein Freundschaftsbund, den ich mit zwei gleichgeplagten Wesen gestiftet hatte. Der eine, ein schlanker zarter Junge, war dem Schneidermeister Heidermann eine Treppe tiefer das, was ich eine Treppe höher Herrn Fintlein war. Der andere, der Pflegsohn einer gewissen Madame Müller, ein blonder Krauskopf mit treuherzig-blauen Augen und roten Backen, wohnte uns gegenüber. Wir wussten uns auf unsern Berufswegen zu begegnen; da ging denn die eine Hälfte des halben Stündchens, das wir zu erübrigen wussten, mit Klagen über die Gegenwart, die andere Hälfte mit Träumen in die Zukunft hin. So sassen wir einst, während unsere Tyrannen uns im Schweisse unsers Angesichtes glaubten, ganz gemütlich beisammen. Einige noch unbesetzte Buden und unausgepackte Kisten – denn es war gerade die Ostermesse – verbargen uns vor jedem Späheraug', das unsere Musse unsern Tyrannen hätte verraten können. Wir sassen auf unsern Holzpantoffeln zu ebener Erde und schauten träumend in das helle Frühlingsgewölk hinein, das eilend über uns dahinzog."

In light of certain noticeable differences in the five narratives in *Die wahrhaftige Geschichte von den drei Wünschen* it would seem that Ludwig wished to have each of his narrators express himself in a characteristic style. Unlike the narrator of *Zu stille Liebe*, the first *Literat* speaks without pathos in a straightforward, concrete, and unadorned manner. We admire both the vividness and the succinctness of his beginning. The background is quite clearly defined: we see the empty booths, the crates waiting to be unpacked, the boys squatting behind them in their wooden shoes, and the bright spring sky overhead with its rapidly moving clouds. We also gain a great deal of information: that the narrator began as a master-bootmaker's delivery boy; that he was dissatisfied with his occupation and longed to do something worthier of his potentialities; that he stole away whenever he could; and that he shared the stolen moments with two young friends who were equally discontent with their lots and who helped make life a little more bearable by sharing his dreams. The neat articulation of the paragraph is also a pleasing quality; and because it is so well articulated its tempo, too, is agreeably rapid.

In *Die wahrhaftige Geschichte von den drei Wünschen* there are several well composed passages such as this one; but within the context of the story their overall effect is unfortunately that of making us even more painfully aware of the cluttered style and the poor articulation of the story as a whole. At the same time, however, they are evidence of Ludwig's steady progress as a narrative writer, for there are more of them in this story than in the earlier works. They are, of course, even more interesting as examples of the complex process by which reality-oriented literature gradually developed out of romanticism in Germany during the third and fourth decades of the nineteenth century.

CHAPTER IV

## THE TURNING POINT
## *MARIA*

For Ludwig's fourth story a number of possible sources have been suggested,[1] but none of the evidence cited warrants our doubting his statement, in a letter to Tieck,[2] that the idea for it came from an anecdote related to him by his friend Wetzstein. The anecdote, a bit on the scabrous side, is about an unusual sexual adventure in which a young linen merchant becomes involved while on a business trip. When he arrives at the inn where he has planned to stay the night the young man is surprised to find everyone in mourning. Upon inquiry he learns that the young daughter of the inn-keeper has died that very day, and as he pays his respects at the bier of the young girl, who is strikingly beautiful, he is deeply saddened by the thought that now no one will ever know her love. This thought remains with him, and later that night it disturbs him so greatly that he is unable to sleep. An irresistible desire to see the girl again prompts him at last to steal down to the room where she is lying. Three times during the night he is magnetically drawn to her bier, and as he stands there for the third time his impulse becomes so intense that he yields to an unnatural impulse and rapes the corpse. Early the following morning he continues his journey. Approximately two years later he returns to the same inn and, to his astonishment, sees the girl whom he had believed dead sitting in front of the building, very much alive and holding in her arms a child of about two years. The girl, he learns, had actually fallen into a trance from which she had awakened the following day. A few weeks later signs of pregnancy had become apparent. The identity of the father is still a mystery, however, for in face of all inquiries, entreaties, and threats the girl has steadfastly denied having had relations with anyone. The young man, horrified to learn the consequences of his act, asks the girl to become his wife.

From the first sketch for *Maria*, which Ludwig made in Leipzig in 1843 not long after he had heard the above anecdote, we see that from the beginning he was fascinated by the psychological implications of the strange situation it describes. The heroine of his own story, he writes, was to be above all naive and pure. This did not mean, however, that she was going to be a paragon of virtue.

For if he planned to emphasize her integrity, the major part of the story was to deal with her reactions to her strange predicament as a girl who experiences love and passion only *after* she has become a mother! To give the necessary relief to the "*Jungfräulichkeit*" of his heroine he envisioned adding, as a sort of negative counterpart, a second female character who was to be fully as attractive as the heroine, but of a frivolous and irresponsible nature.

Although the preliminary sketch contains mainly plans for developing the character of the heroine, it also reveals that Ludwig was quite concerned by the problem of motivating the young man's rash behavior. He might have known the girl from earlier visits to the inn, Ludwig reflects, but without thinking of her as a woman he could love. In this case her untimely death might naturally bring the sad thought that now no one would know her love. As the young man dwells on this thought, Ludwig reflects further, his excitement could conceivably become quite intense; and if while in this state he should approach the bier he might well be seized by the desire to embrace this lovely form which is so soon to lie in the grave. In the dim light he might even have the illusion that the girl is still breathing, and as he bends over her to verify his impression the nearness of her face, so beautiful in repose, might well heighten his desire and prompt him to yield to a wild urge to bring her back to life by warming her body with his own...

The sketch indicates that the projected story was not only to have psychological interest, but also to be "realistic." To make it seem so Ludwig planned to keep it "active" at all times. His plan for realizing this aim was to allow the characters to reveal themselves through their speeches, gestures, and actions as people in the real world do. This idea marks a new departure in his thinking on the matter of characterization, for we find him contemplating here for the first time the exciting prospect of employing dramatic techniques in a narrative work for the purpose of endowing it with a greater degree of objective reality. From *Maria* on, as we shall see, the use of these techniques was to become standard practice.

When Wetzstein read Ludwig's sketch he expressed doubt that a good story could be developed out of such raw materials. His lack of enthusiasm caused Ludwig to drop the project for a while, but he had every intention of working on it during the summer of 1843. In August of that year, however, he moved to Dresden, and the many activities in which he became involved there made it impossible for him to resume work on his story for several months. He finally completed it in December, as we know from an entry in his *Hauskalender*. What Wetzstein had believed impossible Ludwig had accomplished: out of a simple anecdote he had created a work of art.[3]

Ludwig first submitted his story to Heinrich Laube who was still editor of *Die Zeitung für die elegante Welt*. Laube rejected the story, not because he did not like it, but, as Ludwig explains to another editor, because certain things in it caused him to feel that his readers, who were mostly ladies, might be offended by parts of it. Ludwig had no better luck elsewhere. In face of these refusals he felt that his only hope was to interest some influential person in his work, and finally, after much hesitation, he overcame his natural reluctance and sent his manuscript to Tieck with a covering letter requesting that the latter write a preface to the tale, if he should find any merit in it. In his gracious reply Tieck carefully skirted the matter of the preface, and as far as we know he never wrote it. Berthold Auerbach also responded coolly to Ludwig's request to help him in placing his story, and after this cool response Ludwig made no further effort to have it published. It did not appear in print until 1891 when Adolf Stern included it in his edition of Ludwig's works.

The setting of *Maria* is contemporary Germany, and, like Ludwig's first three stories, it also begins in the midst of a conversation. We at once note something different about the opening scene, however, for unlike the beginning sequences in the earlier stories, which take place against the merest suggestion of a backdrop, the first scene in *Maria* takes place in a fully developed landscape which Ludwig obviously wishes us to feel as plastically real. The scene depicts a leavetaking, its main purpose being to inform the reader that young Georg Eisener is about to take a long journey which his father hopes will cure him of some of his sentimentally romantic notions about life. Herr Eisener and his son accordingly figure most prominently at first. The third figure in the landscape, Eisener's friend Ritter, is silent until after Herr Eisener has left, but when he begins to talk he proves to be quite eloquent. The conversation between the two friends exemplifies beautifully both Ludwig's new method of revealing character through dialogue and his new concern for structure; for not only does it tell us something about the two as individuals; it also sounds for the first time the central motive of the story, that of the "virgin" birth. One detail cited here, Eisener's near-sightedness, is of particular significance later; but by bringing it out here Ludwig also realizes two immediate artistic purposes. His main reason for speaking of it is, of course, to motivate Ritter's detailed description of the village of Marklinde, the pastorate, and the surrounding countryside, which Eisener cannot see as well as his friend can; but by allowing Ritter to describe the landscape instead of doing it himself he also realizes his aim of keeping his story "active" and "objective."

From Ritter's detailed description of the landscape, which recalls of the paintings of Waldmüller, Richter, and Von Schwind, we move on, as in an art gallery, to another charming tableau in which we see Maria for the first time. As in the opening sequence, here, too, character is revealed through gesture. We see Maria in a situation in which all of her finest qualities are apparent. She is taking care of a group of children (like Charlotte when Werther first sees her), and her manner of relating to them at once suggests her gentleness and tenderness and her great capacity for loving. Young Eisener is immediately drawn to her, and Ritter, sensing his friend's interest, rounds out the picture, as it were, by warning Eisener that Maria is still a child emotionally in spite of her seeming maturity.

The other scenes in the story are also conceived as tableaux. In each the compositional arrangement seems to have been worked out with great care, and in some Ludwig even uses light and shadow effects in order to bring into relief the persons and objects portrayed. This new attempt to represent reality plastically without doubt reflects his association with the painters and sculptors whom he came to know after his arrival in Dresden. Henceforth we find him experimenting ever more extensively in the application of the techniques of painting and sculpture to narrative writing. In the *Romanstudien* later he even observes that almost all of the techniques employed by sculptors and painters could be used with equal effectiveness by writers.[4]

In *Maria* we feel Ludwig's new "painter's eye" not only in the compositional arrangements, but also in the landscapes. A few, to be sure, reflect the soul-states of the characters as in romantic tales; and in some he personifies nature as in his early stories. We find, for example, gentle evening breezes making music in the trees and morning zephyrs playing games of colors by turning leaves inside out! But we also find what we might call "objectively drawn" landscapes which attest not only to his growing desire to make things seem real, but also to his increased skill in making them seem so.

The action in *Maria* centers around young Eisener and Maria, but since the former is away on a trip during most of the story it may be said to have only one main character. It is divided into three books. The first, which covers a period of a few weeks, introduces us to the hero and the heroine and depicts the unusual circumstances by which they are first drawn together. When we compare this part with the sketch we note many striking differences, most significant of which is Ludwig's manner of dealing with his heroine's "unconscious conception." For in the final version of the story the love-act occurs not while the heroine is on her bier, but while she is in a somnambulistic trance. Young Eisener, who is near-sighted, we remember, does not recognize Maria when she wanders into his room, which is lighted only by the moon's rays; and when his charming visitor undresses and climbs into his bed he naturally does not hesitate to make love to her. After his rash act he is far more conscience-stricken than his counterpart in the sketch and is more determined than ever to make amends when he learns that his nocturnal visitor was *Maria*, whom he loves. On his way to the pastorate, however, he learns, to his great sorrow, that Maria has died that very day. Book I ends at this point. Book II, covering a timespan of three years, brings the account of Maria's vicissitudes as an unwed mother and of her development from a child into a woman. Book III then fills us in briefly on the adventures of Eisener during the interim and describes the circumstances of the lovers' reunion.

In keeping with his aim of offering an authentic illusion of reality Ludwig tries to make all of the happenings in the story seem probable. At times we feel even that he tries too hard, for his explanations occasionally seem forced. To enhance the illusion of "objective" reality Ludwig also follows the procedure mentioned earlier of allowing his characters to reveal themselves through their gestures, speeches, and actions. In their conversations with one another they also tell us things we must know about their past in order to understand them. Thus it is from Eisener's conversations with Breitung, not from Ludwig, that we learn the strange facts which explain Maria's character.

Most remarkable about this girl, who reminds us so much of some of the heroines of Tieck, Novalis, Hoffmann, and Kleist, is her close rapport with nature. During her childhood, we are told, everything animate seemed to her to have human feelings. Trees, flowers, animals, even buildings, furniture, and articles of clothing possessed for her a kind of human identity, and to communicate with these "friends" she invented a private language which only individuals with great poetic sensitivity were able to comprehend. As she approached adolescense, we learn from Breitung, her rapport with nature became even closer, and it was at this time that the moon began to affect her so strangely. With each passing year this influence grew stronger until at last the moon became her "lover and her longing." From this time on she began to walk in her sleep at the time of the full moon, wandering in search of her "lover," and was in this way led to Eisener.

The most fascinating aspect of Ludwig's highly nuanced portrait of his heroine is his description of her reactions following her awakening from her *Scheintod*. Naive as she is, she is at first willing to believe that her pregnancy is a kind of ordeal sent by God. It is her cousin Julie, her negative counterpart in the tale, who first makes her realize that her conception must have resulted from her having unwittingly given pleasure to a man. As she ponders this she begins to regret not having experienced the pleasure of which her child is the visible fruit. Her regret becomes curiosity, which in turn gradually deepens into a longing to know what such pleasure must be like; and in her unconscious mind this nascent desire is from the beginning associated with Eisener, whose image thus becomes that of her ideal lover. By the time they meet again Maria has fallen so completely in love that she is able to move with ease into the role of a mature married woman.

Young Eisener is as naive as Maria when we first meet him. The most obvious sign of his immaturity is his sentimental idealism which is reflected in all of his early conversations, as, for example, in his ardent praise of the feminine sex in one of his first meetings with Breitung. In this paean on womanhood, which has an unmistakably Schillerian ring, Ludwig's anti-Schiller bias comes out quite clearly. Eisener's words here and elsewhere in the early sequences of the story are those of a young man who has acquired most of his experience from books. Shortly after this conversation, however, he begins, like one of Ludwig's favorite Goethean heroes, Wilhelm Meister, to learn from real experience, and the lesson is long and bitter. Only after he has suffered the pains of remorse and loneliness, however, does he come to realize what his true values are; and with this realization the romanticism of his youth is overcome.

Most of the other characters in *Maria* play only supporting roles, but even though they are sketched in rough outline we see them so sharply that they seem definite personalities; Maria's frivolous, but charming cousin, Julie, whom Eisener believes for a time to have been his mysterious beloved; the stern and uncompromising pastor who shows no Christian charity toward his daughter when he discovers that she is about to become a mother out of wedlock; Breitung, whose neurotic, nagging wife has made him something of a misogynist, but who, because he is a skeptic, can help young Eisener to a more realistic view of the world and of human relationships; Rosine, the sharp-tongued spinster with a heart of gold; the pathetic little Johannes, an appealing Oliver Twist type who has known nothing but unhappiness until Maria takes him briefly to her heart; and Eisener senior, the successful mid-nineteenth century business man, the pragmatist with both feet on the firm ground of reality, the skeptic to whom all idealism is suspect, but who, for all that, is sensitive enough to appreciate true beauty and quality.

The crowd scenes reflect a similar sharpness of vision and a similar ability to create an impression of plastic reality. A striking example is the description of a group of people hurriedly seeking shelter during a sudden thunder-shower (W, I, 210-11): "Auf der Strasse unter seinen Fenstern eilten Obdachsuchende in groteskem Aufzug, Tücher oder Teile der untern Kleidung über den Kopf gezogen, aufgeschürzt, so hoch man es mit der Notwendigkeit entschuldigen zu können sich getraute, mit sich allein hinreichend beschäftigt oder einen Teil seiner Sorge Kindern, Alten oder dem Vieh zugewandt, das man eilig einem Torweg oder, konnte man diesen nicht schnell genug erreichen, dem ausgebreiteten dichten Laubdach einer Buche zutrieb oder -zog, im Vorbeieilen nach Temperament oder augenblicklicher Stimmung Tracht und Eile an sich oder den andern belachend, klagend oder fluchend."

Delightful though it is in itself, this animated scene has not been introduced into the tale merely as a comic interlude. Ludwig presents it, significantly, not as something which anyone might have witnessed, but as something which young Eisener sees, and, moreover, as something which he sees at a particular time. By so doing he relates it at once to the action of the tale. The incident occurs shortly after the strange love-night which, because it happened so mysteriously and affected him so profoundly, is still foremost in Eisener's thoughts. He remembers, moreover, not only his pleasure, but also the profound feeling of remorse which overcame him immediately afterward for having taken advantage of his mysterious visitor. As he stands with his forehead pressed against the pane, looking down into the street, he sees the crowd with one eye only; the other, Ludwig tells us, is turned inward on his guilt-filled heart. As he stands thus, absorbed in his own thoughts, the helter-skelter movements of the shelter-seekers below seem to correspond to the confused searchings of his own heart: "...dort Flucht und Verwirrung wie hier." Seen through the eyes of the young hero this incident has not only objective significance as a bit of observed reality, but also subjective significance in the sense that what is observed seems to correspond to the troubled state of mind of the viewer. The scene might thus be said to exemplify both Ludwig's newly acquired ability to endow his works with a feeling of plastic reality and his growing skill in weaving the various threads of his narrative into a harmonious pattern.

Even the individual sentences in *Maria* reflect Ludwig's new skill in imparting a vivid visual impression. I cite as an outstanding example the brief sentence in which Ludwig describes the old gentleman taking leave of young Eisener after having revealed to him the shocking news that Maria has died that day (*W*, I, 214): "Der Alte wünschte eine gute Nacht und trippelte die Stufen, die unter einem schiefwinkeligen Vorbau von ungeschälten Stämmen und halb ausgewaschenem Lehm in sein Häuschen führte, hüstelnd hinauf." In this sentence, each noun, verb, adjective, and adverb functions as a direct stimulus to the reader's various senses, and the total picture evoked by these several stimuli is skillfully framed, as it were, by the rhythm of the sentence as a whole which binds it in this way into a unit of sensory experience.

Both the central problem of *Maria* and the frequent instances of *Zeitkritik* which we find in the story make it clear that Ludwig intended it to be not only a realistic work, but also a moral one. Examples of *Zeitkritik* are numerous. The contemporary German theater comes in for a drubbing, for example, at the hands of the stranger whom Eisener meets in Dresden after his return from abroad (*W*, I, 262). An even sharper commentary on the times is the episode in the village church which Eisener and a young artist friend have decided to visit because of the art works which it contains. The two friends arrive on a Sunday, just after service, and shortly after they have entered the church they hear someone begin to speak in a monotonous tone in the sacristy. Their curiosity aroused, they draw nearer and, as they peer in, discover to their great astonishment that the speaker is not a cleric, as they had supposed, but a village official who is auctioning off various articles, including the doors of the church! Even as they watch one of these is sold, and the new owner calmly lifts it out of its hinges and carries it off. The shocked reaction of the two friends makes clear the intended symbolic significance of the episode, for both feel in this moment, Ludwig tells us, as though Christianity had ceased to exist and as though the Church, having outlived its usefulness, were being sold at auction, bit by bit. Ludwig's moral concern appears most strikingly, of course, in his depiction of the process by which Maria and Eisener gradually acquire the experience and wisdom necessary for leading a well-integrated life. For both the evolution to wisdom is a long and painful process. Both, too, must learn from bitter experience. Their reward for enduring the trials which life offers them is the rich one of self-discovery. From the experiences which they undergo they gain a degree of maturity which enables them to look forward with confidence to the future, whatever vicissitudes it may hold.

Although *Maria* may be considered a moral work in this sense, Ludwig's chief purpose in writing it seems to have been not to point out a moral, but to reveal the process by which the two main characters gain their new insights. This emphasis on psychological processes causes the story to seem closer in spirit to *Die Heiteretei* and *Zwischen Himmel und Erde* than to the earlier stories. We can accordingly speak of it in a double sense as a turning-point. For in it we not only find Ludwig moving toward a new kind of realistic writing based on the "norm" of human experience; we also find him anticipating in various ways the "vertical" conception of character which typifies his later work as a narrative writer.

CHAPTER V

## DIE BUSCHNOVELLE
## AND THE PROSE FRAGMENTS

In August of 1843 Ludwig's Uncle Otto died and left him a small legacy. Now at last he was able to look forward to a life in which he would not have to depend entirely on the sale of his writings in order to exist, and the assurance of a steady income also allowed him to hope that he might soon realize his dream of a home and family. The following year he met the right girl. While on an outing with some Leipzig friends in the spring of 1844 Ludwig had discovered in the Triebisch valley a charming and secluded village called Niedergarsebach which immediately appealed to him because it reminded him of the country around Eisfeld. Feeling that he could work there without distractions and also live there inexpensively, he engaged a room for the summer in an old mill. Early in June he returned, and while strolling one day near one of his favorite haunts he met an attractive girl who was walking with her father. Shortly after this first encounter Ludwig met them again, and this time he introduced himself. It was love at first sight, and by the end of the summer he and the girl, whose name was Emilie Winkler, were engaged. In Ludwig's *Buschnovelle*, which he wrote that summer, we find a charming portrait of Emilie, for she is the prototype of the heroine, Pauline; and from his letters to her during their long engagement (she waited seven years) we also receive a most favorable impression. It is touching to hear Ludwig express again and again his gratitude for her sympathy and understanding and for her infinite patience.

From an entry in Ludwig's *Hauskalender* we know that he finished *Die Buschnovelle*, which he first entitled *Das Buschmärchen*, on June 27, 1844. In July he submitted it to the periodical *Die Rosen*, which promptly rejected it. Two years later he again tried to have it published, sending it this time to *Die neue illustrierte Zeitschrift* in Stuttgart which was sponsoring a prize contest. The story won the prize, but the editors, instead of notifying Ludwig of this fact by letter, printed the announcement of the award in the correspondence section of the periodical where it escaped his notice. When he saw his story in print he of course immediately wrote to request his honorarium. During the interim, however, the periodical had changed hands, and the new editors refused to honor obligations incurred by their predecessors. The royalties were never paid.

Although Ludwig called the published version of his story a *Novelle* we feel that his original title, *Das Buschmärchen*, would have been more appropriate, for the tale reads like a fairy-story in modern dress. Its heroine, an orphan named Pauline (who is really of aristocratic birth, as it turns out) meets a count (in disguise) who falls in love with her, rescues her from the clutches of an ogre-like usurer who holds the mortgage to the old mill in which she lives, and finally carries her off to his castle, where the two live happily ever after. We even find the familiar fairy-tale motive of enchantment and redemption through love, for when Pauline first meets her count he is languishing under a spell of dark melancholy into which he has fallen after a series of disillusioning experiences. She is able to free him from his "spell" because she is willing to prove her love by undergoing a dangerous ordeal which almost costs her life.

*Die Buschnovelle* is an eminently personal work. Both the hero's disillusionment and his longing for love reflect Ludwig's own feelings before Emilie Winkler came into his life; and Pauline's self-sacrificing love also had its real-life counterpart in the selfless devotion which Ludwig found in Emilie. Knowing this we are all the more surprised to find the story so unconvincing, for somehow it never seems to come to life. We are also rather astonished to find it so poorly made after the technical advances which we noted in *Maria*. Its plot is hackneyed, its characters are stereotypes, and it has no real point. It suffers in addition from sentimentality and prolixness. Its most serious shortcoming, however, is looseness of structure. The great number of details which Ludwig crams into its pages all but cause the fragile framework of the story to collapse, and by retarding the reader's progress they also cause him to feel the tempo as too slow. Of the fourteen chapters only the first two move rapidly.

If the trite plot, the uninteresting characters, and the faulty structure of *Die Buschnovelle* disappoint us after *Maria*, Ludwig's other prose works of the 1840's clearly reveal that he was not only developing a new aesthetic viewpoint, but also steadily improving his skill as a narrative writer. In the late 1830's and early 1840's, we remember, a number of new figures had begun to appear on the literary horizon, both in Germany and abroad, and from Ludwig's notebooks we know that several of these writers – Immermann, Gotthelf, Auerbach, Hebbel, Dickens, George Eliot, Balzac, and George Sand, to name but a few – had impressed him profoundly. By this time his own concern with current political, social, and economic questions had already brought him closer to actual reality than he had been before, and the works of Immermann, Gotthelf, Dickens,

Eliot, Balzac, and Sand served now as a kind of added impetus to seek the subject matter of art in contemporary reality. From the mid-1840's on we accordingly find him moving ever farther away from the romantic outlook and frame of reference which had in such large measure determined the form and content of his early works.

Ludwig's new aesthetic orientation is already apparent in the plans and sketches for the series of novels which he planned to write during the 1840's. These projected novels were to range quite widely in subject matter, as the titles mentioned in the notebooks indicate – *Klaus und Klajus. Ein Roman von einem Schulmeisterleben, Die neue Undine, Der neue Don Quixote,* and *Der Kandidat* (sometimes referred to as *Der Apostel*) –, but they were to have two very important qualities in common: all of them were to reflect contemporary life, and the subject matter of all was to be drawn from Ludwig's own experience.[1]

Of *Klaus und Klajus*, which was to be a humorous work, we have in published form only two fragments, *Aus einem alten Schulmeisterleben* and *Das Märchen vom toten Kinde*.[2] The first describes an adventure of Klaus's while in the company of some itinerant musicians who are to play at a country wedding; the second is a romantic *Kunstmärchen*. The principal character of the first fragment is Beust, a Thuringian farmer, who has contracted for his daughter, Rosemarie, a marriage with a man whom she does not love. Everything has been planned for the ceremony and the feast, but on the eve of the wedding Linkenfried, the man whom Rosemarie really loves, but of whom her father disapproves, returns unexpectedly from America, where he has become wealthy, and once again asks Beust for the hand of his daughter. The latter, who prides himself on never changing his mind, jokingly declares that he would give his consent only if the impossible should happen, that by some strange circumstance Rosemarie should fail to be present on the morning of her wedding. This crude joke inspires Linkenfried with the idea of abducting the bride-to-be. The searching party finally discovers a bridal wreath on the banks of the Elbe; and when, later in the day, news arrives that a corpse wearing a wedding dress has been found in the river, Beust concludes that his daughter must have drowned. Even in face of this tragic possibility, however, he determines to proceed with the wedding banquet according to plan. While the feast is still in progress two strangely garbed figures appear who are, of course, Rosemarie and Linkenfried. The hour appointed for the wedding having passed, Linkenfried reminds Beust of his agreement of the previous evening. Contrary to all expectations, Beust, far from manifesting joy at seeing Rosemarie alive, falls into a rage, disinherits his daughter for having deceived him, and promptly marries a rich widow who is one of the wedding guests.

There is a boldness and earthiness about Ludwig's portrayal of peasant life which would have shocked Immermann and Auerbach and perhaps even Gotthelf. We are spared no unpleasant details. Ludwig does not shrink, for example, from showing us the schoolmaster leading his drunken companions into the courtyard "wenn einer sich expektorieren wollte," and at another time we see them sprayed with manure water as a practical joke. At the wedding banquet we are almost revolted by the callousness of the bridegroom-to-be who immediately after hearing of his fiancee's death downs a huge meal!

We find the same earthy realism in some of the scenes of the second fragment, *Das Märchen vom toten Kinde*. We do not know when Ludwig conceived the idea for this little tale, but in his notebooks for the year 1845 there is a poem treating the same theme which would seem to indicate that the idea occurred at that time. The final draft was doubtless completed early in 1846.[3] From the sketches we know that the *Märchen* was to constitute chapters 7-10 of the first part of *Klaus und Klajus*, but there is no mention of what its function was to be in the novel. It begins with a lively scene in which we see two groups of harvesters working on either side of the boundary line between their two villages. With a sweep of his scythe one of them suddenly uncovers the body of a little girl. Her corpse is lying in such a way that her head is on one side of the boundary line and her feet on the other. The reaction of the peasants is surprising, for they seem to feel no compassion at all. Their only apparent concern is which community must bear the expense of burying the child. Two roguish lawyers incite the quarreling groups to institute legal proceedings against one another. While the wrangling is still going on, however, one peasant notices a medallion which is partly concealed by the child's collar, and, thinking that it might be valuable, he offers to bury the child himself. He is foiled, however, for the medallion proves to be worthless. When he no longer has hope of any gain the covetous peasant abandons the child. At this point the tale becomes a *Märchen*. Word of the child's death has meanwhile reached the animals whom she has befriended in life, and they now bury her with infinite tenderness. Their leader, the dog *Jäger*, mounts guard over her grave.

Since Ludwig's notebooks do not indicate what function *Das Märchen vom toten Kinde* was to have in *Klaus und Klajus* we can only judge the story on its own merits. We wonder, first of all, why Ludwig called it a *Märchen*, for it differs strikingly from both *Volksmärchen* and *Kunstmärchen*. The talking animals are the only suggestion of the wondrous, and we miss, too, the element of poetic justice. The world of *Das Märchen vom toten Kinde* is a bleak world where kindness and charity appear not to exist at all. The only characters with human feelings are the animals! The title is unfortunately not the only thing to which we take exception. One of the gravest faults of the story is its sentimentality, particularly in the closing sequences; and it is also clumsily made. The only indication that it is a work from Ludwig's mature years is the manner in which he has represented reality in certain scenes. The description of the harvesters at the beginning is a good example of his ability at this point to create a convincing illusion of reality. The first sentence offers a sweeping panoramic view of the whole crowd of harvesters ("Ein bunter Schwarm von Knechten und Mägden hatte das Tal mit frühestem erobert und erfüllte es mit frohem Lärmen.") Each adjective and noun in this sentence transmits a direct sense impression, and the active verbs set the whole into motion, as it were. In the ensuing sentences Ludwig guides the reader's eye from focal point to focal point in the busy throng of workers ("Dort hatte man das Gras gehauen, hier stand das Heu bereits aufgeschobert; dort kamen schon die Wagen, das gestern Gehauene in die Scheuer zu bringen. Da floss Schweiss, da stieg Duft, und mit den fröhlichen Stimmen der Heuer wettkämpften die Vögel auf Erlen und Weiden, die dem Bächlein in zwei grünen Reihen rauschend und nickend durch das ganze Tal hin das Geleit gaben.") and by so doing involves him directly in the scene. He sees, hears, feels, and smells what is happening.

In the portraits of the characters we sense a similar conscious attempt to impart an impression of tangible reality. All are presented in action wherever possible. We see Hans combing his hair and hear him nervously clearing his throat before he enters the pastorate to try to persuade the miserly minister to preach a free funeral sermon. We note, too, that when he and the other characters speak they use the vernacular forms which would come most naturally to them. All of these touches reveal Ludwig's developing skill as a narrative writer. By this time, it would seem, the working out of the individual aspects of his imaginary worlds no longer posed any serious problems. What he still had to master was the far more difficult skill of integrating the parts of his works into structural wholes which his readers would find authentic.

For the subject matter of the novels which he hoped to write Ludwig planned to draw upon contemporary reality and upon his own experience as in *Klaus und Klajus*. Thuringia, the region he knew most intimately, seemed the logical setting; and he envisioned the series as a whole as a kind of mural of Thuringian life and folkways. The larger problem of unifying the series was to be solved by interconnecting the novels in various ways, but he is not very specific about these in his sketches. The fragments he has left are the only evidence as to how successful he might have been in realizing his ambitious aim, and this evidence is slight indeed. Certain passages in them reflect, to be sure, his best qualities as a writer: his humor; his skill in creating characters, particularly peasant types and eccentrics; and his moral concern. But they also reveal his greatest weaknesses, particularly his tendency to be overly sentimental and his love of detail for its own sake. The latter fault would doubtless have been a most serious handicap, had he ever attempted to carry out his vast project.

Because Ludwig's weaknesses are so much more in evidence than his good qualities in the prose fragments they cannot be rated very highly as artistic achievements. They do have significance, however, as evidence that the mature works of the 1850's were not created spontaneously, but were the natural products of a period of incubation and maturation which extended over more than a decade.

CHAPTER VI

## TWO SCENES FROM PROVINCIAL LIFE
### *DIE HEITERETEI*
### AND *AUS DEM REGEN IN DIE TRAUFE*

The futility of Ludwig's various attempts to have his plays produced, his financial worries, and the general uncertainties of the times after 1848[1] caused him to wonder again seriously at this point whether it might not be wise to assure himself a steady income by becoming a teacher or librarian. In May of 1849 he went so far as to inquire how much capital would be needed in order to open a small lending library in Dresden. Success, however, was closer than he realized. During the summer of 1849 he had completed the final revision of his play *Die Wildschützen*, which he had now decided to call *Der Erbförster*, and he had sent it off at once to his friend Eduard Devrient, the renowned actor, who had offered to help in any way he could with criticisms and suggestions for making it more easily stageable. Devrient was so enthusiastic that he immediately decided not only to use his considerable influence to have the play produced, but also to play the leading role himself. In September came the good news that the Dresden Court Theater had accepted the play. Rehearsals began shortly after Ludwig's arrival in Dresden in late September, but the illness of the leading lady caused the premiere to be postponed until the spring of the following year. One of the most colorful accounts of the opening night on March 4, 1850, is that of Ludwig's friend Moritz Heydrich, who attempts to convey an impression of the play's impact by likening it to a gathering storm whose majesty, as it built up, filled all present with awe, and whose great flashes of lightning and claps of thunder, when it finally broke, caused all to shake with terror. Heydrich also found the play true to life in spite of its supernatural elements and even attributed much of its impact to its unique mixture of romantic and realistic elements.[2]

Following its Dresden premiere *Der Erbförster* was staged in Weimar and Vienna, and these successes opened the way to all of the other important stages in Germany.[3] Almost before he could realize it Ludwig had become a celebrity. One of the many honors now accorded him was an invitation to become a member of the exclusive Dresden *Montagsgesellschaft*, all of whose members were artists, writers, composers, or outstanding professional men. At the meetings of the society he came to know a number of stimulating people, but the most important of his new Dresden acquaintances were Gustav Freytag and Berthold Auerbach, both of whom he had met earlier in the year at the premiere of Freytag's *Graf Waldemar* at the Court Theater. Both were to become devoted friends, and the latter was also to become an important mentor.

Both Ludwig's success as a dramatist and his growing dissatisfaction with life as a bachelor led him finally to disregard all practical considerations and to marry. He and Emilie were married in a simple ceremony on January 27, 1852. Limited means obliged the couple to live in cramped quarters, but the happiness of married life had even so the effect of buoying up Ludwig's spirits. With the help of Emilie, who copied his manuscripts and served in addition as both audience and critic, Ludwig rapidly finished the third draft of the Biblical play which he had begun before his marriage. The final version, which he entitled *Die Makkabäer*, proved to be good theater and was well received at its premiere on January 9, 1853. The success of the play inspired Ludwig to resume work on his Agnes Bernauer-drama, *Der Engel von Augsburg;* but since two versions of the Agnes Bernauer story were currently playing in Germany Auerbach urged him to postpone work on the drama and to write a story instead. Ludwig followed his friend's advice.

The story which he wrote during the fall and winter of 1853-54 was a *Kleinstadtgeschichte* with a Thuringian setting, and he doubtless modelled it consciously after the *Dorfnovellen*[4] which were then finding such favor with the reading public. He entitled it *Die Heiterthei*, naming it after its heroine. From Ludwig's sketches (*W*, II, 331-349) it is possible to follow quite closely the process by which the world of *Die Heiteretei* came into being.[5] In the earliest sketch the heroine, as yet unnamed, was envisioned as a poor girl, no longer in her first youth, who has worked hard to keep herself and her sister's illegitimate child and has known little joy in life. Although near the age where a girl becomes a spinster, she was to have no desire to marry because of her memory of her mother's unhappy married life. As a strong, healthy girl capable of much hard work she was to feel completely self-sufficient. Only one man, a bachelor of forty-two named Hanns, was to interest her at all, but in order to conceal her secret attraction from him and the other villagers she was to scorn him outwardly. Because of the girl's obvious qualities Hanns, whom Ludwig planned to portray as a man anxious to make a fresh start in life, was to be irresistibly drawn to her and was to seek her out constantly in spite of her scornful attitude. At the same time, however, he was to attempt to hide from himself the true depth of his feelings by insisting both to himself and to others that his only motive in wanting to see her is to break her defiant spirit. Between these two individuals blinded by pride Ludwig planned two major encounters, which, because of the ambivalent nature of their feelings for one another, were to become contests of strength. In the first encounter Hanns was to be victorious, but after having vindicated himself as a man in the heroine's eyes he was to allow her to win the second contest. After the first contest the villagers were to side with the heroine; but in the second one Hanns was to be injured, and this fact was to turn the whole town against the heroine. By this time, however, Hanns was to be deeply enough in love to persist in his suit. The way to an understanding was to be provided at last by a child-intermediary, the heroine's sister's illegitimate child, whom both she and Hanns love dearly.[6]

Even from this brief summary it is clear that the main outlines of the action of *Die Heiteretei* were worked out at quite an early point in the genesis of the story. The later sketches thus consist in the main of plans for adding additional incidents and for developing the psychology of the characters. We find only a few brief indications as to how the story was to be narrated, but the sketches do clearly indicate that it was to be a humorous work. For if the characters were to be "borniertest" and "naivest" and the kind of people who take everything too seriously, including themselves, their story was to be narrated with "gemütlicher Ironie" and "drolliger Wichtigkeit."

In the final version of the story the heroine acquires both a name, Annedorle, and a nickname, *Die Heiteretei*, and the hero not only receives a new name, Fritz, but also becomes several years younger. A number of new episodes are added, and the love story is much more fully developed, particularly in its psychological aspects. We also note, to our delight, that the structure of the story has been worked out with great care even though the sketches reveal no great concern with the problem of form. The tale is divided into twenty-three parts of varying length which might be thought of as chapters; but actually the story consists of three main parts. In the first part, which closes with the encounter of Annedorle and Fritz on the lonely bridge in the dead of night, and which fills approximately one third of the total number of pages, events and situations are presented largely as they are experienced and interpreted (or rather misinterpreted) by the heroine. The second part, a kind of flash-back, gives us the other side of the story, as it were, by recapitulating these same events as reflected in Fritz's consciousness. Having had the benefit of both of these accounts of the same series of events the reader at this point is better informed than anyone in the story as to what has happened, and both his awareness of his superior knowledge and his natural feeling of suspense cause him to watch with unusual interest the final unraveling of the complications in part three.

If the imaginary world into which the reader is introduced in *Die Heiteretei* seems a more convincing illusion of reality than the earlier worlds created by Ludwig, this impression certainly stems in part from the fact that in writing it he drew to such a large extent on personal experience. To make the imaginary village of Luckenbach seem as real as possible he reproduced in it several of the structures of his native Eisfeld, and for the speech of its inhabitants he borrowed heavily from the Eisfeld dialect.[7] Luckenbach is, however, neither Eisfeld nor any other German town, but a composite picture, part of whose elements are drawn from Thuringian towns which Ludwig knew, and part of which he simply created out of his own imagination. The same is true of the characters, none of whom has any one prototype in reality.[8]

Although the various details taken over from actual reality make it apparent that Ludwig was most anxious to make Luckenbach seem as real as possible to the reader, he seems on the whole more concerned with giving a picture of the inhabitants of the town than of the town itself, which seems to exist largely as a kind of backdrop against which the characters act out their lives. And all do act out their own lives. We have thus the impression of actually seeing them and of hearing them speak. We even come to know them in the same way that we come to know real people. They seem strange at first, when we first meet them, but as we hear them speak and watch them make characteristic gestures they gradually become familiar. We come to know Annedorle and Fritz even quite intimately, for we see them not only in their day-to-day relationships, but also in the moments when they are alone with their thoughts.

The principal advantage of the dramatic method of characterization as Ludwig employs it in *Die Heiteretei* is, of course, that it makes the story seem far more objectively real than it would have if he had simply narrated it himself as something which he had heard or observed. But by using these techniques in a particular manner he also achieves another important artistic effect. Almost two thirds of the story, we recall, is narrated as the experience of Annedorle and Fritz, and the effect of presenting the reality of the tale in this manner as the experience of the two main characters is to bring the story as a whole into unusually sharp focus. For presented in this way every aspect of the reality of the tale seems to relate in some way to the two main characters and to their problematical relationship, which is Ludwig's central concern.

This attempt to achieve sharpness of focus is evidence that *Die Heiteretei* was put together with considerable care. Further evidence of Ludwig's careful planning of the structure is the skillful manner in which he builds the tale out of the individual episodes. For each scene prepares in some way for what follows, and the work seems thus to grow and develop in an almost organic way. In *Die Heiteretei* we have for the first time in reading Ludwig's narrative works the impression that not a single scene could be deleted without undermining in some way the structure of the story as a whole.

The opening sequence exemplifies both Ludwig's manner of characterization and his close attention to the matter of structure. The main function of the scene, of course, is to introduce Annedorle, whom we come to know here through her remarks, gestures, and actions as a warm-hearted, completely unaffected girl who, because she has abundant vitality and is a tireless worker, has managed to get along well enough up to this point even though she earns very little and has heavy responsibilities as the guardian of her sister's illegitimate child. Later in the scene she also has occasion to express her views on marriage, and after hearing these and witnessing her triumph over the tailor, the smith, and the weaver (which represents for her, we are told, a victory over the entire masculine sex) we also gain some initial insight into her deeper problems, particularly her fear and distrust of the opposite sex. The scene is thus used not only for the purpose of exposition, we see, but also fulfills an important function within the overall structural design of the story by introducing one of the principal motives. The subsequent scenes reflect a similar concern with the relationship of the parts to the whole.

This concern is also apparent in Ludwig's depiction of nature in *Die Heiteretei*. Whereas in the earlier stories the nature descriptions often stand out like pictures which are too large for their frames, in *Die Heiteretei* each harmonizes with the compositional arrangement of the scene in which it occurs, whether it serves simply as a backdrop, or whether it is employed for some subtler purpose such as providing an appropriate background for a poetic or melodramatic moment. In almost every instance Ludwig achieves this feeling of integration by the device already noted, that of depicting reality not as something objective, but as something experienced by the characters, as though he were applying in composing the story the well-known psychological principle that people normally relate reality to themselves and hence always color it somewhat with their own subjective feelings about it.[9]

Another device which Ludwig employs to impart a greater feeling of structural unity and compactness is the *Leitmotiv*.[10] Although he found numerous examples of the *Leitmotiv* in the works of Goethe and also in the works of many of the other writers whom he used as models, from his later remarks in the *Romanstudien* it would seem that it was from Dickens that he learned most about its use as a structural device. All of the studies dealing with Dickens' influence on Ludwig[11] touch on the similarities between Dickens' and Ludwig's use of the *Leitmotiv*, particularly as a characterizing device, but the best known comparison is doubtless that of Oskar Walzel in *Das Wortkunstwerk* (Leipzig, 1926). Walzel finds in Dickens' novels three main types of *Leitmotive* which he distinguishes from one another according to function. The first type is the *Leitmotiv* whose only function is to enable the reader to "recognize" a character whenever he meets him. He likens this type to a "visiting-card" which the character presents when he "calls." An example would be the very distinctive names which Dickens assigns to his characters (Dartle, Murdstone, Chuzzlewit, Bounderby, etc.). A more important group of *Leitmotive*, Walzel finds, are those which relate in some way to the larger moral purpose of the work. An example of this type would be the motive of miserliness as associated with Ebeneezer Scrooge. Walzel's third category includes all of the *Leitmotive* which Dickens uses as structural devices. Examples of this type are the *Leitmotive* in *Hard Times* which not only identify the characters, but also suggest through them the larger social and moral issues of the times – problems such as the dangers of pragmatism or the exploitation of the working class – which are Dickens' main concern in the novel. Of these three types Walzel finds, surprisingly enough, only "visiting-cards" in Ludwig's stories. It is true that Ludwig does employ *Leitmotive* for this function in all of his narrative works. Yet in *Die Heiteretei* and also in *Zwischen Himmel und Erde*, as we shall see, there are also many examples of the other more subtle uses of *Leitmotive* which Walzel praises in Dickens. The "Hier sitz' ich und sag'" of the *Gringelwirts-Valtinessin* is a *Leitmotiv* of the "visiting-card" variety, for it has no influence whatsoever on the course of the action and relates in no essential way to the larger moral significance of the tale. Annedorle's phrase, "Ich brauch' keinen, ich kann's noch selber," on the other hand, is clearly an example of the second, more dynamic type of *Leitmotiv*. The phrase is used initially as a "visiting-card," to be sure, but as we come to know Annedorle we soon see that it does not mean what it says, and that what she proclaims with such apparent self-confidence actually contradicts what we now know to be her most basic inner feeling, her intense longing to be loved. When we have understood the phrase in this sense we see that it is in reality quite closely related to the larger moral theme of the work and hence not a mere "visiting-card." An outstanding example of the third type of *Leitmotiv* is Ludwig's use of the verb *spinnen* in the tale. The verb is associated, quite aptly, with the *Weberin*, one of the great ladies of Luckenbach, who, as a compulsive talker, loves to "spin" out tales. In the important sequence in which the great ladies of the town work out their plan for protecting Annedorle from Fritz, however, we see that the verb is much more than a "visiting-card." For here, before our very eyes, the ladies weave a veritable fabric of intrigue out of the threads spun out by the *Weberin*. One could scarcely find a better example of Ludwig's ability to use the *Leitmotiv* for a variety of different effects, for the "fabric" of intrigue woven by the assembled women not only characterizes them as vicious gossips, but also builds great suspense in the reader, who waits tensely to see what will come of these "spinnings."[12]

Ludwig's use of personal experiences, his objective method of characterization, and his attention to the problem of structural unity all contribute toward making *Die Heiteretei* a more convincing illusion of reality than any of his earlier stories. Throughout the tale, however, we sense that his ultimate aim is something beyond mere verisimilitude, important though that aim was. What causes us to feel this is his obvious attempt to endow the situations of the story with symbolic meaning. The situations involving Annedorle's cart offer a striking example. The basic significance of the cart, of course, is that it suggests the arduous way in which the heroine must earn her living. Early in the story, however, it begins to acquire additional symbolic significance. It first figures prominently, we recall, in the sequence toward the beginning of the tale in which Annedorle succeeds in pushing it out of the mire after the tailor, the smith, and the weaver have tried and failed. Through its association with this feat, which to Annedorle, we recall, symbolized her superiority over all men, the cart, as something which she alone is able to manage, becomes even more than before a symbol of her self-sufficiency. Later, however, in the climactic scene on the bridge, it acquires quite different associations; for here the same cart which had once symbolized her superiority over all men almost becomes the instrument of death for the man she secretly loves when, in her fear that he plans to harm her, she uses it to push him from the bridge into the stream below. Still later, on the day before the wedding, in the scene where Fritz demonstrates his ability to move the heavily laden cart which everyone else is unable to budge, it again figures prominently in an important situation; and here it takes on even further significance in the sense that Fritz's ability to move it suggests the role he will play henceforth in Annedorle's life as one who will be able both to share her burdens and to fend for her at all times. Other examples of "symbolic" situations abound: Fritz's disorderly shop which suggests his dissolute way of life before his reform; Annedorle's house which reflects both her personality and her changing fortunes; the brawl in the inn which symbolizes Fritz's break with his past; the bridge where Annedorle and Fritz meet for the second time which, as a bridge, suggests the bridge of understanding which they have been unable to build between themselves up to that point;

and Fritz's rebuilding of Annedorle's ruined house, which suggests one of the main moral themes of the work: that man is not made to live alone. The cumulative effect of these poetic "overtones" is to add another dimension of meaning by imparting to the story a higher poetic significance beyond its literal meaning.

Although *Die Heiteretei* is a story about small town life, it resembles in many ways the *Dorfnovellen* which were written in Germany from the mid-1830's on. One is accordingly tempted to compare it with some of the contemporary *Dorfnovellen*, both from the point of view of its content, as an expression of an aspect of German provincial life, and from the point of view of the technical devices which were used in order to make the image of reality seem convincing. Because those who wrote *Dorfnovellen* chose so many different regions as their settings, and also because they did not share the same view of peasant life, their works perforce differ considerably in spirit and outlook. To discover in what respects *Die Heiteretei* is typical we must, therefore, compare it with several *Dorfnovellen*. Four representative, yet sufficiently diversified examples at once suggest themselves: Karl Immermann's *Der Oberhof*, because it is a sort of archetypal form of the genre; Annette von Droste-Hülshoff's mystery story, *Die Judenbuche*, because it is both a classic example of the *Novelle* and an outstanding example of the kind of "poetic realism" we find in *Die Heiteretei*; Jeremias Gotthelf's *Elsi die seltsame Magd,* because of Ludwig's great admiration for Gotthelf, and because it, too, is a story about false pride; and Berthold Auerbach's *Barfüssele*, which seems an obvious comparison, both because Auerbach was Ludwig's friend and mentor and because in the *Romanstudien* Ludwig specifically refers to this story as an example of what the *Dorfnovelle* should be. As points of comparison I selected the following qualities: the use of autobiographical materials; local color effects; what one might call "sociological" concern; the use of objectifying techniques, such as quoting from documentary sources or employing the dramatic method of characterization; general philosophical outlook; and the degree to which the work was consciously conceived as a "value-experience."

Although these *Dorfnovellen* of course differ from one another, sometimes quite radically, in form, content, and *Weltanschauung*, it is nevertheless clear that Immermann, Droste-Hülshoff, Gotthelf, Auerbach, and Ludwig employed quite similar techniques for making their tales seem convincing illusions of reality. Those common to all would include: drawing to the largest possible degree upon personal experience; objectifying the work by narrating it in such a way that the reader has the illusion of seeing and hearing what is happening; and planning and executing the structural design so that the work seems to grow and develop naturally in terms of a concealed causality, like an organism growing in nature. All seem to have believed, too, that the best means of creating a convincing illusion of reality is to allow the characters in a story to lead their own lives. By "activating" their stories in this way all of them were also able to realize another desirable artistic effect, that of causing the moral meaning to seem to grow naturally out of the situations represented. A further point of resemblance is the similarity which we note in the style-level of the stories. In keeping with the simplicity of the characters and the situations the style in all is relatively simple and unadorned.

Although Auerbach was not altogether pleased with *Die Heiteretei*,[13] out of loyalty and affection for Ludwig he did his best to help him find a publisher. His second attempt was successful; the story was accepted by the *Kölnische Zeitung* and began to appear on December 5, 1855 in the *Feuilleton* section under the title, *Die Heiterethei. Eine Kleinstadtgeschichte von Otto Ludwig*.[14] Two publishers subsequently offered to print the story in book form. The offer of the Meidinger Verlag in Frankfort-on-the-Main was the more attractive of the two, and on April 28, 1856 Ludwig sent off his manuscript with a covering letter promising a preface and a companion-piece to be entitled *Aus dem Regen in die Traufe*. The volume containing the stories appeared the following year and was announced as the first in a series of studies on Thuringian life to be entitled *Thüringer Naturen. Charakter- und Sittenbilder in Erzählungen von Otto Ludwig*.[15]

*Aus dem Regen in die Traufe* is the account of an ill-fated amorous adventure of Herr Bügel, the diminutive tailor whom we remember from *Die Heiteretei* as a swaggering fellow who is always trying to convince his neighbors that he is master in his own house even though the whole town knows that he is completely under his mother's thumb. The story begins with a description of the house on the outskirts of Luckenbach which the tiny tailor, now a man of thirty, shares with his mother. We enter the house by way of the stall under the living-room, and as we pass through on our way upstairs Ludwig points out a tiny room adjoining the stall where the Bügel's housemaid, Sannel, sleeps. The location of the room at once suggests the humble position which the girl occupies in the household, and its extreme tininess, a quality which Ludwig underscores, suggests at the same time that its occupant must be an almost elfin-like creature.

In the living-room we find Sannel and Frau Bügel who are waiting up for the little tailor. The latter's angry glances at the switch which hangs so menacingly over the platform where her son works at once suggest the abnormal relationship which exists between her son and herself, and Sannel's occupation – she is mending with loving care a pair of tiny socks – also suggests the role which she plays in the little tailor's life.

The following scene, which depicts the return of the tailor and his two cronies from the fair, is also an "action" scene, and here again Ludwig succeeds in imparting through the gestures and speeches of the characters everything that the reader is supposed to know about them at this point. By skillfully focusing our attention on certain aspects of the little tailor's appearance and behavior he is able to give us both a vivid first impression of his tiny hero and considerable insight into some of his deeper-lying problems. For the details which he calls to our particular attention – the tailor's abnormally large sideburns, his boastful manner, and his swaggering walk – are all expressions of an inner need to compensate and thus suggest, even while we laugh at them, what a problem it is for this little man to assert his manly ego in a world where everyone, including his mother and most other women as well, is larger than he.

In striking contrast to the little tailor's self-confident manner in the presence of his cronies is his entrance into the house where he claims to be undisputed master. Here again certain details are highlighted – the fact that he crawls through a loose plank in the fence rather than entering by the gate, and the fact that Sannel is waiting to help him –, and here again they are symbolic, suggesting both his inferior position in his own home and the important role which Sannel plays in his life as an ever-ready helper and comforter.

In the following scene with Sannel, in which, significantly, the tailor speaks in an almost inaudible whisper, we discover another rather surprising reason for his bragging manner. For as we watch Sannel reacting to his account of his exploits during the day we realize that she has in some measure encouraged this trait in him by praising him as she does and by justifying everything he says. She is thus, we see, not only a friend and comforter, but also a sort of magnifying mirror in which the little tailor sees an enlarged and quite flattering image of himself. We see here, moreover, that Sannel not only encourages him to live in a world of illusions, but also supports him in his belief that others are unfair because they fail to appreciate as she does his superlative qualities.

This scene brilliantly exemplifies both Ludwig's skill in employing dramatic techniques for character portrayal and his ability to create symbolic situations. For here the whole situation "means." The grouping of the two figures, with the tailor enveloped in the folds of Sannel's skirt, suggests the latter's protective role; and both her carefully shaded lamp and the subdued tones in which the two speak suggest their fear that Frau Bügel may hear them. At the same time the scene as a whole reveals the pathetic disparity between the tailor's real situation in his home and the sensation of power and magnificence which he enjoys here in the company of the only person who ever takes him seriously.

The little tailor's fear of his mother prepares us to meet a dragon, and we are accordingly surprised to discover that she is not nearly as dreadful as we had imagined. For as we come to know her we learn that her domineering attitude is not simply the expression of a desire to rule, but a natural outgrowth of the extreme solicitousness which she has always felt because of her son's diminutive size. If her motive has been positive, however, the effect of her overly-protective attitude has been totally negative, as we soon see. For by shielding him she has stunted his growth as a personality, and by dominating him she has caused the main ambition of his life to become the purely negative one of getting out from under her thumb as soon as possible. His strategy is to marry a girl who is both bigger and stronger than his mother, and the heart of the tale is the account of what happens when he tries to do this.

Ludwig originally planned to have his hero find the desired qualities of size and physical strength in a poor female relation. Once sure of her catch the girl was to prove to be an even worse tyrant than the mother, but in the nick of time a traveling journeyman was to take her off the hero's hands by marrying her himself. Later, however, he had the much happier inspiration of a triangle in which the tailor's fiancée (who is not a relative in the final version) becomes interested in the journeyman, whom she believes to be wealthy, while the latter is attracted to Sannel. In addition to enhancing the plot-interest of the story this change also offered a means of punishing the villainess instead of rewarding her (she is tricked into leaving the Bügel's house by the journeyman's false promise of marriage) and an opportunity to deepen the psychological portrait of the hero by giving him an occasion for jealousy. In the final version the tailor's jealousy is actually a necessary step in the development of his love for Sannel, for, self-centered as he is, he is unable to realize how important she is in his life until he thinks he is about to lose her.

The tyrannical regime of the tailor's fiancée (whom Ludwig refers to simply as *Die Schwarze*) is a difficult ordeal for the entire Bügel household. Yet the experience also results in an important gain in the form of the new understanding which comes about between Frau Bügel and her son. For when the little tailor explains to his mother at the height of their troubles that it was only his desperate desire to be free which drove him into the arms of *Die Schwarze* she realizes how wrong she has been and promises never to be domineering again. With the clarification of the problematical relationship with his mother and the elimination of *Die Schwarze* through the kind offices of the journeyman all of the obstacles in the way of the tailor's happiness are removed, and all ends well. He marries Sannel, who adores him more than ever after having almost lost him; his mother keeps her promise; and the experience of true contentment enables him finally to stop compensating. With time he becomes one of the most esteemed members of the community, we are told, and the tale concludes with the delightful observation that all of his children were of normal size.

The fact that the hero of *Aus dem Regen in die Traufe* is also a character in *Die Heiteretei* is but one of a number of links between the two stories, for they resemble in many ways in form and content. The most obvious similarity, of course, is that both are comic works. In writing them Ludwig has observed one of the basic principles of the psychology of humor: that a situation tends to seem comic only insofar as the spectator is emotionally detached from it. His technique for preventing the reader's emotional involvement and for keeping his point of view "objective" is beautifully illustrated in the opening scene of *Aus dem Regen in die Traufe* where he objectifies his little hero almost to the point of making a caricature of him. By so doing he conditions us at the very beginning of the tale to respond to him as a comic figure. Having established this pattern of stimulus and response he can safely introduce a more serious note, for we are prepared to smile henceforth whenever we see Herr Bügel. In the ensuing scenes we are accordingly amused by many things which would not seem funny at all if the little tailor had been introduced to us as a serious character. On the other hand, since Ludwig does not wish us to forget that Herr Bügel's family situation is a serious one, the story becomes a comic work with serious implications. The balance which he attempts to maintain between the comic and the serious is quite a delicate one, but he succeeds admirably. We find the same delicate balance in *Die Heiteretei*. There, too, Ludwig wishes us to feel a warmth toward Annedorle and Fritz even as we smile at their foibles. Like Herr Bügel, they accordingly never seem clowns whose sole purpose is to amuse us.

There are numerous other points of resemblance between *Die Heiteretei* and *Aus dem Regen in die Traufe*. In both stories Ludwig attempts to portray convincing characters living in logical relationships with one another in a seemingly real environment, and in both, too, he obviously wishes not only to show us *how* things are in the world of his tale, but also to give us some basis for understanding *why* they are so. Another similarity is the fact that Annedorle, Fritz, and Herr Bügel are all "problematical" individuals; and the moral purpose of the two works is also essentially the same: to demonstrate how an individual can achieve a better perspective on reality and how, in light of this, he can make a better adjustment to life. We note, too, that Ludwig depicts this process in the same manner in both stories by allowing his characters to "act out" their conflicts and to arrive at their own solutions.

A far more significant parallel than any of these, however, is the fact that in both *Die Heiteretei* and *Aus dem Regen in die Traufe* Ludwig portrays his principal characters as individuals rather than as representatives of a general human condition, attitude, attribute, or emotion. We feel the individuality of Annedorle, Fritz, and Herr Bügel at all times, not only in their speeches and actions, but also, as we noted, in the manner in which they experience reality. We sense it keenly, too, in their aloneness. By emphasizing the individuality of his main characters Ludwig not only makes them stand out sharply as characters; he also causes us to feel that each of them is important for his own sake. They become thus meaningful for us not for what they represent, but for what they are. This conception of character is not only interesting in itself, as a reflection of the kind of heightened awareness of the importance of the individual which Ludwig shared with so many of the writers of his generation,[16] but also as an expression of the new conception of the relation between the particular and the universal in art which developed out of that awareness. Considered from this latter point of view the individuality of the characters can be cited as one of the qualities which most clearly mark *Die Heiteretei* and *Aus dem Regen in die Traufe* as nineteenth-century works, for one of the basic differences between the German nineteenth-century writers and their literary forebears is the tendency of the former to portray characters as individuals rather than as representatives of general human types or of abstract ideas. Thus, in addition to their intrinsic merit as fine examples of Otto Ludwig's mature narrative style *Die Heiteretei* and *Aus dem Regen in die Traufe* also possess literary historical interest as outstanding examples in the domain of comic writing of the nineteenth-century notion of the relation between the particular and the universal in art.

CHAPTER VII

## ZWISCHEN HIMMEL UND ERDE

Since we have neither notes nor sketches for *Zwischen Himmel und Erde* we have no clear picture of the genesis of the work, but from the rough draft of one of Ludwig's letters to Keil, the editor of *Die Gartenlaube*, who had written to Ludwig that he would be happy to have him contribute a story, it would seem that he wrote it during the late summer and fall of 1855.[1] Ludwig's hope that his story would appear in *Die Gartenlaube* may be the reason why he broke it up as he did into twenty-three parts, for the breaks, which are not designated as chapters in the final version, would have been convenient dividing points, had the story come out as a serial. It seemed almost a certainty that it would, for *Die Gartenlaube* had already announced it as a forthcoming publication. After having seen the manuscript, however, Keil, who had expected a much shorter work, decided not to publish it. This was a bitter disappointment, for Ludwig had been counting on the money, but fortunately another possibility presented itself early in 1856, when Meidinger wrote from Frankfort on-the-Main that he was willing to consider the story for publication in book form. Happily he did not share Keil's feelings about the work, and by April it was already in press.[2] Today it is generally regarded not only as a masterpiece of fictional writing, but also as one of the most significant landmarks in the development of literary realism in Germany.

In one of the many passages on narrative techniques in the *Romanstudien* Ludwig remarks (S, VI, 100-101) that a writer of fiction may tell his story synthetically, analytically, or by a combination of these two methods. In practical terms this means that he has three alternatives: he may begin with a situation out of which complications subsequently develop; he may place the main antecedents of the action before its actual beginning in such a way that the story becomes the resolution of prior conditions; or he may employ a combination of these techniques. In writing *Zwischen Himmel und Erde* Ludwig seems to have chosen the third of these alternatives. For if his story begins analytically, in the sense that at the beginning everything has already happened, very early in the tale a series of flashbacks take us back to a situation out of which quite serious complications develop for all of the main characters; and from this point on he uses a combination of the analytic and synthetic methods as he gradually reveals the circumstances and the hidden causes which explain how things came to be as we see them in the opening scene.

The opening sequence reads something like the description of a stage-set. In it we see only outer surfaces – the outside of the Nettenmair house, the outside of the adjoining structures, the outside of the neighboring houses. The only hint of anything beyond the surface is Ludwig's remark that there is something almost disturbing about the extreme orderliness and cleanliness of the Nettenmair garden, which seems to have been brushed rather than raked. This remark suggests that the garden must in some way "explain" the old gentleman whom we see sitting in it on this Sunday afternoon, but we learn nothing further here about the psychological implications of the old man's compulsive neatness. Of him, too, we see only the outer surface here.

It is actually quite appropriate that in the opening scene we should be shown everything from the outside only, for one of the most important things we learn about the old gentleman whom we meet in it is that his life has always been a closed existence about which even those nearest to him have known very little. By mentioning at this point the curiosity of the townspeople about Herr Nettenmair Ludwig stimulates our curiosity as well, and we, too, begin to wonder why he never married his widowed sister-in-law after her husband's tragic accident so many years ago. Our suspense is heightened when Ludwig remarks that this atmosphere of Sunday calm has not always prevailed here, and that wild emotions – pain because of stolen happiness, frantic jealousy, and bitter mistrust – once held the inhabitants of this house in their grip. To give us a foretaste of what we will experience when we hear about those dark days Ludwig suddenly increases the degree of pathos at this point by introducing Shakespearean comparisons into his style. Thus we hear of "murder casting its dark shadow into the lives of these people" and of "despair moving about at night, wringing its hands."

The function of the opening sequence, which consists of ten paragraphs, is to locate the story in time and space and to tell us what we need to know about the world in which the characters live. The details are thus not neutral or accidental; they have been purposefully selected as essential historical antecedents. Ludwig even underlines the significance of some by personifying them: the Nettenmair house "opens" its shutters to "look out" on the street; the house opposite seems to "disdain" the Nettenmair house, and so forth. The modern reader may well feel inclined to smile at these personifications, but they serve nevertheless to impress deeply on the reader's memory the objects with which they are associated. By personifying them Ludwig also makes them seem to imply more than they represent. We sense thus even in our first contact with them that they are elements among which certain effective relationships exist which will become evident later, relationships which exist in connection with these elements alone and with no others in the world, and we look forward to learning what these relationships are. Our overall impression of the setting, as it is sketched in this brief ten-paragraph introduction, is that it is an important focal point to which the tale will in all probability return from time to time.

Having thus impressed his setting upon our minds Ludwig is ready to begin the main part of his tale. The past up to this point has been carefully shrouded in darkness. It comes back now in the form of memories awakened in old Herr Nettenmair's mind by the sound of the bells of St. George's, for the bells had pealed in the same way when he returned home from Cologne thirty-one years earlier in reply to his father's summons to help with the repair work on St. George's roof. At that time, Ludwig tells us, the entire future of the young slater had been connected with the slate roof of the church. Now, however, he sees there only his past. Once again we sense a shift in the narrative perspective as Ludwig suggests here that as he sits in silent reverie listening to the sound of the bells the old man may be remembering what happened in this garden and in this house. For a time it seems as though Ludwig might be going to narrate his story from old Nettenmair's point of view from this point on, for the second part begins with the remark that by turning back the pages of memory (pages which can, of course, exist only in Nettenmair's memory) we find a young man before us instead of an old one. The technique which he employs, however, is to alternate between direct narration and interior monologue. Thus the tears which fill the eyes of the returning traveler are described by Ludwig; but the young man's feeling that he would have wept, had he not felt ashamed, is his own feeling, as is his impression that his entire sojourn in Cologne has only been a dream. Because so much of what happens in *Zwischen Himmel und Erde* goes on in the minds of the characters Ludwig uses the device of the interior monologue quite frequently in the story, and in every instance he uses it in combination with direct narration as he does here. It is Ludwig himself, for example, who supplies the information at this point that Apollonius' brother Fritz will also be helping with the repair work on St. George's roof.

The use of the present indicative in this sequence heightens our feeling of the immediacy of what is transpiring. We seem to relive these memories with Apollonius. We feel ourselves climbing with him the little hill which still hides his home town from view, and we see it reappear in the same manner that he does, first the tower of St. George's, then the roof of the church, and finally the whole city spread out below. As he looks down on his father's house we are again permitted to read his thoughts, and we learn that he is troubled by the antipathy which his sister-in-law Christiane feels for him. His momentary brooding provides the motivation for a second flash-back which illuminates an incident which occurred shortly before his departure for Cologne, thus taking us back an additional five years in time. As he looks back on this incident, which happened during a dance on the Eve of Pentecost, Apollonius, who was then himself in love with Christiane but too timid to tell her so, does not yet realize that at that very ball his brother, while pretending to act as his intermediary, had begun his own courtship of Christiane. In this poignant moment we gain a degree of insight into the relationship between the two brothers which Apollonius himself does not have at this point, and what we learn helps us to understand the tension which later develops between them.

Having turned back the clock thirty-six years in as many pages – what has been narrated up to this point occupies about one seventh of the total number of pages – Ludwig begins his account of the complicated relationships which developed in the Nettenmair household after Apollonius' return from Cologne. Although the story moves forward in a fairly unilinear fashion from this point on, Ludwig continues to employ the combination of analytic and synthetic techniques which we mentioned earlier, a procedure which he later described as that of illuminating step by step a bit of the riddle in such a way that at every stage in the forward progress of the action light is shed on some aspect of the past which is still shrouded in mystery.[3]

The panoramic view in the scene depicting Apollonius' return from Cologne is the only view Ludwig gives us of the small provincial city in which the action of *Zwischen Himmel und Erde* takes place. Henceforth we see only the Nettenmairs' house and St. George's church, the two points between which the action alternates. We never learn the name of the town, and we also hear nothing about the larger political, social, and economic background of the times. Nor are we told the year in which the story begins. The two main "sets" are described in considerable detail, however, and these we can visualize quite clearly.[4] It is actually not necessary for us to know more than Ludwig tells us about the physical surroundings, for the emphasis in the story is not on events, as we soon see, but on the revelation of character. As the tale proceeds it becomes an ever more searching analysis of the three main characters.

Ludwig himself thought of *Zwischen Himmel und Erde* as a

realistic work; yet we find in it many qualities which we more commonly associate with romantic writing. The most flagrantly romantic element is doubtless the mysterious "Geist des Hauses" which hovers about spreading an atmosphere of gloom, and which seems quite anomalous in a work which is otherwise so close to everyday reality. Some of the landscapes also seem romantic, particularly those which reflect the mood of the characters.

Also suggestive of romantic writing is another quality which has not been sufficiently pointed out: the musical quality of the composition. In using the term "musical" here I mean, of course, not the art of producing harmonious or melodious sounds, but the higher skill of combining musical themes into compositions of definite structure and meaning. Ludwig does just this with the motives he employs in *Zwischen Himmel und Erde*, for he develops and combines these with one another as though they were musical themes. We think, for example, of the bells of St. George's church which we first hear pealing at the beginning of the tale, and which acquire, as the story progresses, an ever increasing number of associations for the hero. For a time they become even the voice of his conscience in the sense that whenever they strike two, as they did at the time of Fritz's fall, they recall both his brother's death and the guilt which he has felt ever since because he wanted to have his brother out of the way. Another striking motive is the epithet "der blaue Rock" which is applied both to old Herr Nettenmair and to Apollonius, and which suggests not only the many similarities between father and son, but also, through these, the powerful forces of heredity and tradition which we see operating in such an inexorable way in the tale.

From the point of view of both the structural design and the higher meaning of *Zwischen Himmel und Erde* the title-phrase might be said to be the most important motive in the story. In the story proper the phrase first occurs in the initial description of the slater's trade just before the beginning of the main action. In this passage (46-49) Ludwig "explains" the symbolism of his title-phrase by showing us how he proposes to use the situation of the slater symbolically as a means of communicating some general truths about human life. In doing so he also gives us, interestingly, a clue as to how we should read the work, for what he does here essentially is to suggest that we consider all of the situations of the story as symbolic. A few pages farther on (74) the title-phrase, now already rich in symbolic associations, recurs, this time as an expression of the feelings of Christiane in the wonderful moment when she realizes that she has at last shaken herself free of her old hatred of Apollonius. She is watching her brother-in-law, whom she has just forgiven in her heart, as he ends his day's work on the roof of the church, and in the rays of the setting sun both he and the moving scaffold on which he is suspended seem golden and radiant and free. Ludwig's artful use of the title-phrase here to describe his heroine's inner feelings in this serene moment enables him to suggest to the reader not only Christiane's soaring emotion, but also the lofty position of Apollonius in her esteem. It also enables him to express something else, something of which she herself is not yet aware: the renascence in this wonderful moment of the love which she has suppressed during the years of her marriage. The phrase, now a fully developed motive, recurs most effectively four pages later (79) when Ludwig speaks of the "moving scaffold" of Fritz's thoughts as not being suspended between heaven and earth, but as "rapidly careening downward towards hell."

The main implication of the phrase *"Zwischen Himmel und Erde"* is that human happiness is found in a just balance between the spiritual and physical sides of our nature, since for most human beings happiness is best realized in an existence which is lived in terms of spiritual goals and ideals, but in which worldly pleasures also have their just place. At the same time, however, it is a reminder of human imperfection; for it also suggests that man, as a creature who is *"ni ange ni bête,"* often fails, for this very reason, to achieve the desired balance between his physical drives and his spiritual aspirations, and so fails to make a satisfactory adjustment to reality. In the tense scene in which the irate father metes out justice to his guilty son Fritz, who feels that he bears the guilt of Cain in his father's eyes, the title-phrase recurs with this implication; for although it is evening and the surrounding world is serene in the golden glow of sunset, the peacefulness of the falling evening does not reach these two embittered men. All else in the world is integrated; only they are between heaven and earth (153).

In the closing paragraph of *Zwischen Himmel und Erde*, which points out the "moral" of the story, Ludwig assigns still another meaning to his title-phrase. In the final scene we see Apollonius as an old man once again, for the closing sequence returns us to the initial situation. He is sitting in his tidy little garden, as when we first saw him at the beginning, and at a distance, concealed behind a trellis, stands Christiane. The church bells are still ringing, but now, Ludwig tells us, the sound of the bells, the fragrance of the roses, the song of the hedge-sparrow, the rustlings in the garden, and the roof of the church all seem to express a message which we can also read on the visages of the two old people. What these things seem to say is this: that although men are prone to speak of their happiness or unhappiness as heaven-sent, what they call happiness or unhappiness is but raw material which must be shaped in some way. For heaven does not send man happiness; he prepares his own happiness and raises heaven in his own heart. If we can bring heaven into ourselves, Ludwig continues, we need have no care about going to heaven; and whoever does not carry heaven within himself will search in vain for it through all the universe. A double exhortation follows: that man should use reason as a guide in shaping his life, but not to the detriment of feeling; and that he should not turn away disapprovingly from the world as it is, but seek to do justice to the world. For in being just to the world he will also be just to himself. In this spirit, the passage concludes, man should live his life between heaven and earth.

The sentiments expressed here remind us of the views of the two most prominent German christologists of Ludwig's day, David Friedrich Strauss and Ludwig Feuerbach, for they recall both Strauss's basic tenet, that the unity of God and man is realized not in Christ, but in mankind itself and in the course of human history, and Feuerbach's "anthropological" Christianity, which deifies man and reduces the Divinity to the status of a projection of the highest human attributes. For in Ludwig's remarks, too, we note that the only transcendence expressed is a transcendence in immanence. This brings us to one of the most fascinating things about *Zwischen Himmel und Erde*, that in spite of its religious-sounding title, its Christian symbols, and its moral tone, it is a work totally without transcendence in the Christian sense. Although a church is one of the main focal points of the action Ludwig never shows us its interior; and we also note that religious agents are absent and that the sacraments provided by the church are never mentioned. In their moments of anguish, which are many indeed, the characters receive no help from the church, as far as we know, and there is no mention of their ever turning to a higher being for help. At Fritz's funeral, significantly, the fact stressed is not that he is buried as a Christian after having taken his own life, but that, thanks to his brother's efforts, the hammer on his coffin, the symbol of his worldly profession and status, is untarnished!

The tone of the final paragraph would seem to indicate that Ludwig considered the tale of the two brothers, absorbing though it is, subordinate in importance to the higher moral idea which the story of their conflict is supposed to illustrate, for he is obviously striving there to impart to the tale some meaning beyond its literal one. A higher meaning seems indeed to shine through all the events and situations of the outer action as we consider them in retrospect. The title suggests man's basic situation as a being who must constantly maintain a balance between his physical nature and his higher aspirations; the slater's trade suggests man's exposure to the vicissitudes of life; the church in whose shadow the outer action takes place bears the name of a saint who is one of the most celebrated opponents of evil; and the burning churchtower becomes a kind of summons to self-transcendence. What holds our interest as we read the story, however, is the account of the tragic struggle between the two brothers and Ludwig's penetrating analysis of their characters. In the portraits which he draws we note first how he makes each resemble the father in certain ways. Apollonius has inherited all of his father's positive qualities – industry, conscientiousness, a refined sense of craftsmanship, orderliness, and a highly developed feeling of family honor –, but in him these qualities become almost compulsive. He seems a prisoner of his heredity. After his father's death he becomes the same austere symbol of competence, propriety, dignity, and reserve that his father had been. Fritz, on the other hand, has inherited chiefly his father's negative qualities. Or perhaps one might better say that his father's weaknesses reappear in him as pathological symptoms. For whereas old Herr Nettenmair is only mildly paranoid, Fritz's delusions of persecution and of his own greatness resemble the classic symptoms of paranoia. Fritz admires his father and even tries to be like him, as we see, but he imitates the wrong things. To impress the men he whistles as his father did, only more sharply, and he also coughs more importantly and spits more decisively. Because he imitates only such habits as these, however, and not the qualities which commanded the respect of others, it is clear that he cannot succeed. Yet as we watch him we cannot help pitying him somewhat, for we realize that his negative heredity is in large measure responsible for his failure. His inability to succeed only makes him the more resentful of Apollonius, who is seemingly so easily able always to do what is right; and the latter becomes a thorn in his side. Admirable though Apollonius's actions may seem in the eyes of the world, they come thus paradoxically to have a detrimental as well as a beneficial effect in the sense that they cause Fritz to become ever more cynical, morose, and wretched. Ludwig enables the reader to feel the progressive disintegration of Fritz's personality by recording the changes in one of his most characteristic qualities, his laughter. In the earlier sequences it is "jovial," and as his inner tension increases it becomes in turn "herablassend," "verachtend" and "wild." It is next characterized as "krampfhaft," then as "entsetzlich," and still later it acquires a quality akin to "heulen." At last it is "wahnwitzig." As Fritz's paranoid feelings become more and more intense he becomes increasingly difficult to live with. Thus as the story unfolds we see the brothers becoming in ever greater degree irritants for one another, each driving the other gradually to the point of desperation and ultimately even to violence.

So great is the stress of living in the tense atmosphere of the Nettenmair house that Apollonius also begins to develop psychoneurotic symptoms not long after his return from Cologne. We witness both the "traumatic" experience which makes his illness acute, the death-struggle with his brother, and the after-effects of this experience: hypersensitivity, anxiety, and the strange dizziness which comes over him each time he attempts to climb the tower of St. George's church to finish the repair work which had been interrupted by his fight with his brother. His guilt burden is tremendous, so great in fact that it prevents him, even after he has discovered Fritz's treachery, from enjoying the happiness which is so rightfully his. For him the only possible solution is sublimation.[5]

Fritz's betrayal of Apollonius, Christiane, and his father is, of course, the principal cause of the barrier which separates the main characters of *Zwischen Himmel und Erde* from one another. The strange nature of the father and the two brothers makes it seem doubtful, however, whether even under better conditions they could have reached the kind of understanding necessary for close family relationships, for they simply cannot communicate with one another. The more they try, the farther apart they become. Because they misunderstand each other's motives their feelings, perforce, also become confused, and, misled thus by both their intellects and their feelings, they err gravely in their actions toward one another. The barriers created by these misunderstandings become at last insurmountable. Even after Fritz has been removed from the scene Apollonius and his father fail to reach one another; and because the former's almost pathological sense of guilt prevents his taking the happiness which so rightfully belongs to him, he and Christiane also continue to live in separate worlds. Christiane's attitude in the last scene, as she gazes at Apollonius from behind the trellis, poignantly suggests the loneliness and emptiness of their life together.

Because *Zwischen Himmel und Erde* gives us such a capsuled view of human life the moral passage at the end has a somewhat hollow ring. For the picture of loneliness which it shows us does not correspond to the conciliatory view of human life which the final paragraph proclaims. The final scene, on the other hand, is completely consistent with what has gone before. For having learned the underlying reasons for the isolation of the two main characters we now actually see, in the grouping of the two figures, how they continue to live apart from one another.

If the depth perspective of character in *Zwischen Himmel und Erde* makes it seem modern, both the conception of human nature and the aesthetic outlook reflected in it are nonetheless closer to the classical outlook on life and art. For to create characters such as Christiane, Fritz, and Apollonius, Ludwig obviously had to believe, as the writers of Goethe's generation did, in human integrity, the possibility of human perfectibility, and the freedom of human beings to make moral choices; and from the moral tone of the work it is also apparent that as a creative artist he held similar convictions concerning the power of aesthetic experiences to transform people in some beneficial way. This is actually not surprising, even in light of his criticism of the writers of the preceding generation, for even his anti-Schiller bias was directed not against Schiller's idealism as such, but against what he felt to be its remoteness from actual reality. Among the classical and romantic writers he felt that only Goethe had created idealistic works which were firmly rooted in reality. If contemporary literature was to have value for contemporary readers it would have to be as firmly rooted in reality as Goethe's art, he contended, and it would also have to take into consideration the changed conditions of life, the new ideas on art and reality, and, most important, the new spiritual needs which had arisen as a consequence of these new conditions and attitudes. One very radical change, as he saw it, was the increased pressure of real circumstances on everyone. For his contemporaries, he insisted, the demands of reality had become practically inescapable. One could no longer ignore them and talk about ideal values for future generations whose needs it is impossible to predict. It was now time, he felt, to evaluate, with an eye to their practical value for living, the ideals and attitudes inherited from the preceding age. When he did so he found many inadequate, as he points out in the *Romanstudien* (*S*, VI, 17), because they did not correspond to the changed notions of his day: "Wir haben jetzt ein andres Ideal der Männlichkeit wie der Weiblichkeit, als in der Zeit unsrer klassischen Dichtung, ein andres der Natur – denn in dieser sehen wir nicht mehr bloss die passive Seite –, ein andres Ideal des Erhabnen und des Schönen; nicht mehr die Resignation ist der Grundton unsres Ideales..." Ludwig's last remark here has a particular significance in reference to *Zwischen Himmel und Erde* in that it refutes the view of some critics that Apollonius reaches the classical attitude of *Entsagung* in renouncing Christiane's love.[6] The situation of the two main characters at the end even seems to suggest that in the case of Apollonius and Christiane renunciation was not a commendable value at all, since in their lives its end result has been a needless separation. Ludwig's own explanation of Apollonius's character would seem to indicate that he shared this view, for he states (*S*, VI, 223), that it was his intention to portray his hero as a *Hypochondrist* who reaches the only solution possible in terms of his particular temperament and personality structure.

The new poetic ideal, Ludwig writes in the selection cited above, "...ist auch nicht mehr Predigen von unsern Idealen, Reflexionen darüber, sondern Vertiefung derselben in das handelnde Leben;

konkrete Darstellung derselben." In the stories from *Maria* on he attempted to do this by using bits of real-life experience to illustrate the values he wished to express. His point of departure in these was thus always *Wirklichkeit*, which for him always meant a real situation in actual reality. In *Die Heiteretei, Aus dem Regen in die Traufe*, and *Zwischen Himmel und Erde* it meant even some aspect or aspects of his personal experience. Examples abound in *Zwischen Himmel und Erde*. Some of Apollonius's traits, his stern sense of duty, his idealism, his conscientiousness, his civic pride are traits of Ludwig's own father; and other details in the story also obviously stem from Ludwig's experiences in Eisfeld and other nearby towns. He must have known, for example, the tombstone in Hildburghausen which marks the grave of the slater who, on the night of February 5, 1835, during a blizzard, climbed the town church tower at the risk of his life to extinguish a blaze which had been started there by a bolt of lightning; and doubtless he also knew about the chimney-sweep named Dankmeyer who, after having distinguished himself by his bravery on the night of the fire, refused to accept the purse which the grateful townspeople wished to press upon him.[7]

Because Ludwig considered moral content more important than verisimilitude, however, the stories from *Maria* on became a kind of compromise between reality as he knew it to be from his own experience and reality as he thought it ought to be. This balance between real and ideal was the goal which he set for the "poetic realists" of his own day to whom he looked to build the foundations of the new poetry.

In the preface to the first edition of his unwieldy nine-volume novel, *Die Ritter vom Geiste,* in 1850 Gutzkow proclaims his work as a new form of the novel which he has developed as an attempt to meet the new requirements for narrative fiction in his day. For the modern writer, he states, the old episodic novel, which he calls *"der Roman des Nacheinander,"* is a thing of the past. To present the complex panoramic and synchronic view of reality which he and the writers of his generation wish to impart a new type of novel had to be created. This new art form, which he feels is able to reflect more of the facets of reality and hence is able to offer the reader a more convincing illusion of life, he calls *"der Roman des Nebeneinander,"* and he announces it as the art form of the future. Little did he realize when he wrote these words that some of the leading writers of his day had already progressed beyond the point where even the radically new form of the *Roman des Nebeneinander* was adequate; for some of them, and among them Otto Ludwig, had already become more interested in deepening rather than broadening the vision of reality in their works. As we come now to appreciate more fully the work of Ludwig and others in developing this new depth perspective we see how they, even more than the naturalists, were the true forerunners of such contemporary writers as Hesse, Mann, and Kafka; and as we realize this we regret all the more that the naturalists paid so little attention to them. How much they might have enriched their art by adding the new depth dimension which the mid-century German writers had been developing!

CHAPTER VIII

# FROM PRACTICE TO THEORY
## *DIE ROMANSTUDIEN*

Although the Ludwigs had to live modestly, they were a happy family, and to Ludwig's great delight none of his three children showed any signs of the nervous ailment which had plagued him throughout so much of his life. With each passing year, however, financial problems became more pressing. One of Auerbach's letters to Emanuel Geibel gives us an impression of how bleak the situation was in 1856: "...Dass sich die Sache mit O. Ludwig so verzieht u. nun so problematisch geworden ist, ist schmerzlich. Ich muss Dir aber sagen, dass auch die äusserlich angenehme Form, in der noch etwas geschehen kann, willkommen aufgenommen wird. L's Frau hat in diesen Tagen das dritte Kind bekommen u. er ist noch immer zergrübelt in Bezug auf das Drama u. sein körperlicher Zustand lässt ihn Arbeit von solcher Spannung nicht unternehmen..."[1]

To his friends' credit it must be said that they did everything possible to help and that their efforts were unceasing. At Auerbach's suggestion Geibel approached the King of Bavaria and was fortunately able to persuade him to grant Ludwig a small stipend; and in 1861, thanks largely to the good offices of Auerbach, Freytag, Julian Schmidt and others, Ludwig was awarded the Schiller prize for *Die Makkabäer*.

Almost simultaneously with this improvement in his material fortunes, however, came a very serious set-back in health. For only a few months before receiving the prize he suffered a violent recurrence of the symtoms which had been troubling him off and on since 1840. From this time on the burden of almost constant pain was added to his other cares. In 1860 he was still able to attend an occasional concert or theatrical performance, but from 1861 on he became virtually a prisoner of his illness, which crippled him almost entirely during its intermittent onslaughts, and from which he never was to recover. One set of symptoms would disappear only to be followed by others; and even during the rare moments when he was relatively free of pain he was too listless to concentrate. Creative writing became increasingly difficult. In a letter to Auerbach in March 1862 he voices the wish that he could photograph by some process or other the multitudinous forms which were crowded together in his imagination clamoring for realization in works of art. For, he asks pathetically, how could he hope to realize even the smallest fraction of his many ideas when the slightest exertion produced a veritable avalanche of pain under which he might then lie buried, as it were, for days or even weeks? Over the protest of both his family and his friends he burned a number of his sketches in October 1864, exclaiming that he was simply no longer able to endure having the ghosts of all those unwritten works haunting him at night.[2]

During the last ten years of his life Ludwig devoted most of his energies to critical and aesthetic studies, but even a cursory glance at his other writings from this period reveals that his creative imagination was also active to the end. In the last weeks of his life there came even an unexpected resurgence of physical energy and a brief respite from suffering which enabled him to work out a detailed sketch for a new play. Death interrupted his work on this project on February 25, 1865, just thirteen days after his fifty-second birthday. Even as a fragment, however, *Tiberius Gracchus* is eloquent proof of the freshness and vigor of Ludwig's creative imagination during his last years, and it stands, thus, one might say, as a sort of promise of what might have been, had he had time and energy to express in new works the rich insights won from the long hours which he had spent analyzing other writers' works.[3]

Ludwig's hope in pursuing these analytical studies was that he might be able to discover by a close reading of the dramas of Shakespeare and the narrative works of Scott, Dickens, Eliot, Gotthelf, Auerbach, Keller, and other contemporary writers whom he admired, the timeless, universal rules governing the creation of literary works of art. Since his aim was the purely practical one of discovering new techniques he did not at first think of publishing his studies and accordingly did not organize them in any systematic way as he went along. In the form in which he left them they fill several notebooks and consist of hundreds of aperçus and analytical passages whose only apparent underlying unity is the unity of purpose which inspired them. Heydrich, anxious to make at least the Shakespeare studies available to the public, prepared them for publication not long after Ludwig's death. His edition[4] was a labor of love, but since his editing consisted mainly in arranging the studies in chronological order it is not very useful. Adolf Stern avoided the main shortcoming of Heydrich's edition by sacrificing chronological order and grouping the studies under topical headings[5] He followed the same procedure with the *Romanstudien* which were published for the first time in his edition.

Over the years the *Shakespearestudien* have gradually come to occupy a position of importance in nineteenth century Shakespeare criticism,[6] but the *Romanstudien* are still relatively unknown.[7] Everyone is of course aware that we must turn to them if we wish to know what Ludwig's aesthetic views were during the last years of his life; but what very few people have realized is that, if studied closely, they also offer something else which is rare indeed in nineteenth century critical literature. For considered collectively they constitute a kind of embryonic theory of the novel which is of particular interest as the contribution of the writer who gave currency to the term "poetic realism".[8] The quantity, diversity, and range of the *Romanstudien* at first obscure the fact that they actually deal with a relatively small number of basic technical problems which Ludwig illuminates from several different angles; and since these problems are also those for which he was seeking practical solutions while writing his stories our discussion of them can serve at the same time as a kind of summary of what was said earlier concerning the techniques which he developed for creating his imaginary worlds.

The clearest statement of Ludwig's views on the basic problem of the relation between art and reality is to be found in the essay "Die dramatischen Aufgaben der Zeit" which appears as the first of the *Shakespearestudien* in Stern's edition (*S*, V, 35-61). Reality (*Wirklichkeit*), he asserts here, should always be the writer's point of departure; and he goes on to deplore that so many of his contemporaries were steeping themselves in philosophy rather than studying the world and human nature. Philosophical reflection and artistic creativity were in his estimation two entirely separate processes which an artist could not engage in simultaneously without risking the impairment of his most precious faculty, his innate ability to universalize sense experience through his imagination.[9] His own point of departure, he tells us, is accordingly not the world of concepts, but the real world, the world of men, of passions, and of effects (*S*, V, 39).[10]

In his critical studies Ludwig often reiterates this basic axiom that all art should arise out of real experience, but he also adds as an important corollary that the artist must learn to select for representation in art only the most meaningful aspects of his real experience. For art "...ahmt nur das Wesentliche nach, sie wirft das Zufällige weg. Sie ahmt den Weltlauf nach, wenn sie erfindet, aber in ihm nur das Wesentliche, dasjenige, was sich jederzeit als wesentliches Zubehör ausweist (*S*, VI, 38)." In the form in which they reappear in the completed work of art the details and elements drawn from reality will accordingly resemble but slightly their counterparts in the real world, for the process of mimesis, he felt, is in many ways analogous to that of memory. "Die Poesie," he writes (*S*, VI, 42), "verfährt nach den Gesetzen der Erinnerung; sie ändert nicht, was geschehen, aber sie mildert es künstlerisch."

Art was thus for him always illusion, and he accordingly considered the truth of art as quite different from historical truth.[11] In the *Romanstudien* he even goes so far as to state that the reader or spectator should at all times be aware that what he is experiencing is only an illusion, and in light of this he advises the artist not to attempt too great a degree of verisimilitude. "Die Natürlichkeit und Wirklichkeit," he writes (*S*, VI, 22), "darf nie so weit getrieben werden, dass wir sie nicht mehr mit dem klaren Bewusstsein anschauen, sie sei nur Nachahmung."

Although the *Romanstudien* deal mainly with the technical aspects of the narrative writer's craft, several of the articles also touch on the closely related matter of the differences between the various literary genres. In these articles, too, Ludwig's approach is almost entirely from the practical point of view, however, and his discussions accordingly tend to center around the different techniques employed by narrative and dramatic writers. Since Ludwig was primarily a dramatist and narrative writer rather than a lyric poet, the emphasis, as one would expect, is primarily on the differences between the drama and the novel. One of the most essential differences which Ludwig points out is the tendency of the drama toward a greater degree of abstractness. He attributes this both to the more limited scope of the drama and to the fact that most dramatists concern themselves with universals rather than with particulars (*S*, VI, 84). Because in narrative works, on the other hand, the outer environment plays so much more important a role than in the drama, the novel, he felt, must be conceived in more concrete terms than the drama and must also concern itself more with particulars: "...der Roman aber wird der innigsten Durchdringung des allgemein Menschlichen durch die individuellen historischen Agentien bedürfen (*S*, VI, 84)." He insists for this reason that the setting of a novel should always be a clearly defined world which resembles the real world in all essential aspects. The novel should thus ideally be close to the present: "Der Roman soll nicht isoliert sein vom grossen Geschichtsleben der Welt, er soll auf einem wirklichen Raume in dieser Welt und in einer wirklichen Zeit derselben spielen, und das Allgemeininteressante der Fabel dadurch modifiziert sein (*S*, VI, 84). Ludwig believed that a novelist can best achieve this kind of historical truth by writing from personal experience. If, on the other hand, he should feel himself drawn to some historical subject he should attempt to familiarize himself with the background of the times by reading widely in chronicles and other documentary sources, as the historian does, even consulting, where necessary, geographical, anthropological, and other available accounts of the period and locale of his projected work.

Since the reader feels the effects of the outer environment so much more directly in a novel than in a play the characters in a novel perforce seem more passive, Ludwig believed, than do the characters in a play. To make clear the distinction which he felt he describes dramatic characters as "anthropological types" and the characters in narrative works as "social types": "...die Gestalten des Dramas sind anthropologische, die des Romans sind Gesellschaftstypen. Jene wollen etwas, sie handeln, und dies Handeln Lears u. s. w. ist Lear; bei dem Romancharakter tritt mehr die Existenz heraus...(*S*, VI, 87)." The novelist shows us thus not only individuals and their passions, but individuals as members of confessions and political parties and as representatives of the various social classes, in short as social beings.[12]

From the point of view of Ludwig's narrative works his remarks in the *Romanstudien* concerning the extent to which the novel and the drama may borrow from one another without losing their essential identity are far more enlightening than his observations on the differences between the two genres.[13] Because he was convinced that a realistic illusion depends primarily on the reader's sense of the immediacy of what is happening, and because in his view the best means of imparting this sense was to cause the reader to feel the characters as real people whom he can see and hear, he actually recommended that novelists employ dramatic techniques for the important purpose of making their characters seem three-dimensional. He also recommends using the dramatic method of characterization for another important artistic purpose: that of revealing inner processes in a convincing way. For in real life, too, he points out, people normally express their inner feelings, their conflicts, and their anxieties in some form of overt action, whether a gesture, a remark made to someone, or a dream or inner monologue in which they "act out" their conflicts.[14]

If a novel is to impress the reader as a convincing illusion of reality, Ludwig felt, it is important not only that its characters seem life-like, but also that everything in it should seem probable and logical. One of his prime requisites for the imitative world of the novel was accordingly that every effect in it should be seen to proceed from a logical and plausible cause. In setting forth this requirement, however, he makes due allowance for the fact that other artistic considerations, particularly the author's concern for suspense and the "comfort" (*"Behaglichkeit"*) of his reader, often make it necessary to conceal, for a time at least, some of the connections between causes and effects in a story. "Wir müssen immer das Ziel über dem Wege vergessen," he writes (*S*, VI, 130), "und nur zuweilen daran erinnert werden, um es wieder zu vergessen."

Because this requirement of logical causality necessarily presupposes concern with structural organization we naturally find several references in the *Romanstudien* to the complicated problem of the proper arrangement and disposition of parts in a narrative work. "Ein so grosses Tier wie ein Roman muss ein Rückgrat haben," Ludwig writes in one passage (*S*, VI, 63). The "backbone" might be, he felt, any one of a number of things – the life story of the principal character or characters; an external circumstance around which the action is built; an object or goal to be attained by the characters; a possession to be protected; but whatever its nature, it had to be, in his opinion, a central core to which all aspects of the work relate in some integral way (*S*, VI, 63). His favorite analogies for illustrating this point are the relationship between the branches and the trunk of a tree and that which exists between the organs of the human body and the body as a whole.[15]

Although Ludwig stressed structural organization in narrative fiction primarily because of his conviction that a well-structured work offers the most convincing illusion of reality, an equally compelling reason, he felt, is that the essential quality of suspense (Ludwig uses the more expressive term *"Spannung"*) also depends on the artful arrangement of the parts of a story. Ludwig's many references to *Spannung* in the *Romanstudien* are evidence that he attached great importance to the skill of creating sustaining suspense in a narrative work. The problem of *Spannung* interested him from the point of view of both author and reader, and he accordingly considers it both as a technique and as an aesthetic experience. The function of *Spannung*, as he saw it, is not only to keep the reader between uncertainty and anticipation by breaking off tantalizingly and by concealing the essences of things behind surface appearance, but also – and this he considered far more important – to "direct" the reader's feelings in a certain way by causing him to "long" for the resolution of the complications invented by the author. "Wir [die Leser] werden gewonnen," he writes (*S*, VI, 101), "etwas leidenschaftlich zu begehren," and what we long for is, he feels, a "becoming," a *"Werden."* For a story, he writes at another point (*S*, VI, 97-98), must not only arouse our emotions; it must also set us at rest again, and it is this that we "long" for: "Sie [die Erzählung] muss befriedigen, d. h. diese leidenschaftlichen Begierden müssen in einen harmonischen Zustand der aufnehmenden Kräfte am Ende sich auflösen..." He describes the frame of mind in which it should leave the reader as "ein erhöhtes Lebensgefühl," a heightened "Zustand aller Vermögen, der aber nichts leidenschaftliches mehr hat," in other words a sense of "Gleichgewicht der gesamten Kräfte." From a good story, he concludes, the reader thus has the right to expect both the two subjective conditions of *"Spannung"* and *"Befriedigung"* and their objective counterparts *"Verwicklung"* and *"Lösung."* It is clear from these passages that Ludwig's ideas on the nature and function of *Spannung* in narrative writing are in perfect harmony with his philosophy of literature, for he regarded literature in like manner, we recall, as a controlling and directing of emotions, the aim of which, as he saw it, was to transform the reader spiritually in some positive way.

In keeping with his belief that literature should serve as a school for living Ludwig has much to say in the *Romanstudien* on the role of literature as an educational and cultural force. From the point of view of these functions of literature, he felt, very special problems faced the contemporary writer because of the new ideals of masculinity and of femininity and also because of the new ideas on nature and reality which the new age had brought with it. As a consequence of these new ways of looking at reality, he continues, he and his contemporaries were perforce led to scrutinize closely from the standpoint of their practical applicability the ideals handed down as a legacy by the preceding generation, and they have found these ideals inadequate in the main. His explanation of the radical difference in outlook between the two generations is that his age has experienced reality in a much more direct and dynamic way than the preceding age did. In accordance with this new way of experiencing reality, he concludes, they inevitably developed dynamic new concepts of what is beautiful, lofty, and sublime, and also new human values which have now become the values of their age. The old ideal of resignation, for example, no longer seems to them life's highest wisdom, he maintains, nor are they content, as Schiller seemed to be, to talk about ideals as though they were something apart from reality. The pressures of real living, he continues, have forced him and those of his age to leave behind them forever the paradise of ideal chimeras which the writers of the classical and romantic age depicted in their works; and now, as individuals committed to an active existence in the very real present, they require new active ideals: "Kraft verlangen wir von unsern Idealen, das Abenteuerliche und Hohle, die Geziertheit und lügnerische Attitüde der Selbstbespiegelung hassen wir als Schwäche. Gesundheit, d. h. Naturgemässheit der menschlichen Verhältnisse verlangen wir; keine Helden, die Helden werden durch Beschämung durch Weiber, keine Helden, die sich an den Frauen anhalten; das Weib will den Mann achten (*S*, VI, 17)."

Literature as the ideal medium for representing ideals in action seemed to Ludwig foreordained to play a major role in the cultural life of the new age. Before it could express appropriate practical ideals, however, it had first, he felt, to discover what these ideals should be. He accordingly summons contemporary writers to seek in the hearts of those about them the ideals which exist there in the inarticulate form of mute yearnings and to give form to these inarticulate ideals in their works of art. "Ganz verkehrt ist es," he writes (S, VI, 16), "Ideale einer vergangenen Zeit nachzudichten, die schon ihre möglichst schöne Realisierung in den Gestalten der grossen Dichter dieser vergangenen Zeit gefunden haben; ebenso, ihnen gegenüber bloss negierend, opponierend zu verfahren; vielmehr ist es die Aufgabe, den Idealen, die noch gestaltlos, als blosse Sehnsucht in den Herzen und Köpfen der neu strebenden Gegenwart zittern, die Gestalt zu geben, in der sogleich jeder Zeitgenosse das erkennt, was er hegte, aber nicht gestalten, d. h., nicht anschauen konnte. So lehrte der wahre Dichter seiner Zeit wonach sie sich sehnt, die ideale Form der Menschheit, wie seine Zeit sie fordert – er lehrt ihr ihr Bedürfnis und giebt ihrem Denken und Gehaben das Muster."

To characterize the type of fiction which he believed most appropriate for his age Ludwig employs the term *Volkslitteratur*. The term, as he defines it, refers to a type of writing directed not toward a learned public of connoisseurs and critics, nor toward the kind of intellectual elite to whom Goethe, Schiller, the romanticists, and, in his own day, the *Jungdeutschen* had primarily addressed themselves, but toward the ordinary man of common sense. In order to make this appeal to the ordinary man, he felt, fiction must be about the norm of humanity and deal with real human situations and problems of everyday human life similar to those which the contemporary reader would be likely to confront (S, VI, 179).

Because he believed equally firmly, however, that the reader also has the right to expect spiritual enrichment from what he reads, he also proclaimed it the duty of the writer of fiction to add in some meaningful way to the fund of the reader's experience of life (S, VI, 98) (S, VI, 179). To realize this aim of leaving the reader with an enhanced feeling of life and of his own humanity fiction, Ludwig believed, must be conceived and written in such a way as to seem not only real, but in a sense even hyperreal. To achieve this aim a novelist, he contended, must depict his characters so that they seem different from real people, even though they are life-like, and must impart to the situations in his work a greater degree of universal significance than one would find in any similar situation in reality. The world of the work of art, as he envisioned it, was thus never to be a mere photographic reproduction of reality, but a world which while resembling the real world in all essential ways, also differs from it, particularly in the sense that in it the higher meanings of phenomena are more clearly apparent than in reality.

This is the sort of poetic truth Ludwig describes as his ideal in his celebrated article on "Poetischer Realismus" (S, V, 458-462). From the article we see that in his usage the term meant a heightened, or corrected vision of reality, a vision so constructed that it possesses not only literal meaning, but also a higher symbolic meaning which is immanent in it and which radiates from it at all times. For the "poetic realist," he proclaims (S, V, 458-59), gives us a world, "...die von der schaffenden Phantasie vermittelt ist, nicht von der gemeinen," and this world is a re-creation, "...keine sogenannte phantastische Welt, d. h., keine zusammenhangslose, im Gegenteil, eine, in der der Zusammenhang sichtbarer ist als in der wirklichen, nicht ein Stück Welt, sondern eine ganze, geschlossne, die alle ihre Bedingungen, all ihre Folgen in sich selbst hat. So ist es mit ihren Gestalten, deren jede in sich so notwendig zusammenhängt, als die in der wirklichen, aber so durchsichtig, dass wir den Zusammenhang sehen... eine Welt, die in der Mitte steht zwischen der objektiven Wahrheit in den Dingen und dem Gesetze, das unser Geist hineinzulegen gedrungen ist, eine Welt, aus dem, was wir von der wirklichen Welt erkennen, durch das in uns wohnende Gesetz wiedergeboren. Eine Welt, in der die Mannigfaltigkeit der Dinge nicht verschwindet, aber durch Harmonie und Kontrast für unsern Geist in Einheit gebracht ist; nur von dem, was dem Falle gleichgiltig ist, gereinigt." By creating imaginary worlds of this kind in which all higher meanings are immediately apparent the "poetic realist" attains, Ludwig believed, both the naturalist's aim of objective reality and the idealist's aim of ideal content.[16]

Although Ludwig was aware that many of his German contemporaries were attempting to realize in their fictional works the kind of balance between truth to reality and ideal content which he is talking about in his article on "Poetischer Realismus," he felt that it had been better realized in England by writers such as Scott, Eliot, and Dickens. He praises all three for their consistent efforts to impart to their works a feeling of historical authenticity, for their attention to structure, for their use of dramatic techniques to make their characters seem life-like, and for the moral content of their works. Scott wins particular praise for representing the "norm" of humanity in his *Durchschnittshelden* (S, VI, 114-121) and for his ability to endow even his lengthiest novels with the quality of "epische Schlankheit" (S, VI, 123). Eliot's novels pleased him both because they offer such a convincing picture of contemporary life and because they reflect such high moral purpose. He also admired Eliot's honesty and candor which led her not to cajole her readers, as so many contemporary writers with an eye on the market were willing to do, but to show them life as it is, as an experience which is both beautiful and ugly (S, VI, 170). The numerous articles on Dickens express admiration not only for the latter's skillful use of dramatic techniques in characterization and for the moral quality of his works, but also for his ability to control the pace of his novels so effectively and for his humor. The free intermingling of the serious and the comic in Dicken's novels was for Ludwig one of the most convincing proofs of their truth to reality.

While Ludwig's discussions of contemporary English novels in the *Romanstudien* emphasize the writings of Scott, Dickens, and Eliot it is clear from numerous passages in the various articles that his attitude toward all of contemporary English fiction was on the whole quite favorable. What he prized most highly in the works of his English colleagues was that they reflected to so much greater a degree than contemporary German fiction did the qualities which he felt to be essential for modern fiction: closeness to contemporary reality; characters who resemble real human beings and who live together in logical and plausible relationships; tightness of structure; moral content; and realistic ideals in harmony with the exigencies of contemporary reality. These qualities which endeared the English writers to Ludwig were to him ample proof that in English literature the spirit and vitality of Shakespeare, who was in his eyes the greatest writer since antiquity, were still very much alive (*S*, VI, 65). Higher praise than this he could not have given.

# CONCLUSION

Although Ludwig's narrative works vary considerably in form, style, and content it is possible nevertheless to discern three clearly defined stages in his development as a writer of fiction. The first, the period of *Das Hausgesinde, Die Emanzipation der Domestiken,* and *Die wahrhaftige Geschichte von den drei Wünschen,* might well be called his apprenticeship, both in the sense that he was learning from others and that he was receiving little pay for what he did! The second, during which he wrote *Maria* and the prose fragments, was a period of extensive experimentation in the course of which he became more and more deeply concerned with the aesthetics of literature and with problems of craftsmanship. He continued to experiment during the third phase of his development, the period of *Die Heiteretei, Aus dem Regen in die Traufe,* and *Zwischen Himmel und Erde,* but, since these stories were his masterpieces in the domain of fiction, we might perhaps best characterize this period as the time of his emergence as a mature artist.

If the trivial, derivative stories of the first period seem to have been tossed off in a casual manner this was in part because in those days the only art form in which Ludwig had ambitions of excelling was the drama. Not until *Maria* do we find him taking narrative writing seriously. It is the first story which he consciously wrote as a work of art. It is also the first which focuses entirely on everyday reality. For, unlike the first three tales, in which the action moves at times quite suddenly from the real world into a kind of fairy-tale world, *Maria* never takes us beyond the confines of everyday life and reality. The emphasis is even on the humbler aspects of reality. None of the characters is really exeptional, not even the sleepwalking heroine! All represent the "norm" of human experience. And to make them seem as real as possible Ludwig employs extensively for the first time the device of allowing them to act out their own lives. He also attempts in various ways to make the world in which they live seem objectively real. Structure, too, receives serious attention, for by this time he had already reached the conclusion that only a well structured work is capable of communicating the kind of authentic illusion which he wished to impart.

A similar deepening of artistic concern is apparent in the novel-projects and prose fragments of the late 1840's. Like *Maria*, these works also reflect Ludwig's basic aesthetic conviction that a work of literature should not only amuse the reader but also enrich him by teaching him something worthwhile about human life. Even though this was his principal aim, however, he seems far more absorbed by the problem of imparting a convincing illusion. His belief that this could best be achieved by confronting the reader with life-like characters led him to experiment ever more extensively, in the stories from *Maria* on, with techniques for making the characters seem objectively real. One of the most exciting results of these experiments was without doubt the new method of portraying reality as the experience of the characters. The double advantage of this technique, as we saw in *Die Heiteretei, Aus dem Regen in die Traufe*, and *Zwischen Himmel und Erde*, was that it enabled Ludwig to suggest most effectively both the complexity of reality and the essentially subjective nature of our experience of it. The new "depth-view" of character which it made possible anticipates in a most impressive way the "vertical" method of characterization which we find in so many contemporary novels and stories.

When Ludwig began *Die Heiteretei* he was already convinced that the form of a work of art is something unique, and from this conviction developed a new approach to the problem of structure. For Ludwig, as we recall, *mimesis* meant not the reproduction of forms already existent, but the creation of a new form which resembles living nature in its essential aspects. This is what he means when he writes in the *Romanstudien* (*S*, VI, 38) that true art is "die Kunst, die wieder Natur wird." He sought to achieve this aim in his later stories by endowing them with what he believed to be the essential properties of nature, growth and development. It was his hope that they would seem to the reader to develop in terms of their inner causality and to shape themselves from within as the forms of nature do; and since he felt that such an impression could only be conveyed by a carefully planned structure in which all parts dovetail perfectly, he devoted much time in his later stories to working out the formal design. Among them, however, only the last can be said to approximate the ideal toward which he was working, for only in *Zwischen Himmel und Erde* does the structural organization suggest something of the harmony, consistency, and coherence which we observe in the process of organic growth in nature.

The practical problems with which Ludwig had to cope in pursuing his aim of greater faithfulness to reality in the stories from *Maria* on continued to be his chief concern, as we saw, in the critical and theoretical studies to which he devoted so much of his energy in his last years. For the main purpose of both the *Shakespearestudien* and the *Romanstudien* was, as we noted, to discover by reading other writers' works the technical means which they had devised in order to impart to their works the qualities which he had striven to realize in his own, particularly the qualities of truth to reality, historicity, objectivity, and tightness of structure.

When we compare the world of Ludwig's stories with our own world we are first struck by their extremely limited scope, for they show us only a very small segment of human life and experience. The settings of most of his stories, we remember, are small towns or villages somewhere in Germany, and only rarely does the action move beyond these narrow confines. The events which take place in these settings are never precisely dated, and we rarely feel any connection between them and the larger political, social, and economic life of the times. The stories have thus a certain timeless quality even though they are about contemporary life. The characters are for the most part quite provincial in outlook. There is also nothing exceptional about them. They are people with no special talents or abilities, and their experience of the world rarely extends beyond the borders of their native region. None of them is in any way *dämonisch*. We find among them no Don Juan, no Faust, no Rastignac, no Emma Bovary, no Ahab. Most of them are respectable, law-abiding citizens who are well aware of the difference between right and wrong and who try to live decent lives. All of them enjoy a certain degree of moral freedom, but their lives are determined to such a large extent by the circumstances of their heredity and environment that they seem on the whole passive rather than active, like pawns of fate rather than masters of their destiny. Since all of them are essentially simple people they are naturally not philosophically inclined. Their only means of understanding life, it seems, is to live it, and since this approach perforce involves a certain amount of trial and error they make many mistakes. We sometimes have the impression that they are only muddling through. Most often they are. And their final solutions are always unheroic ones in keeping with their essential mediocrity.

One of the strangest things about Ludwig's characters is that they seem to lack so completely the kind of piety which one would expect to find in people of comparable social and cultural backgrounds. None of them, overtly at least, manifests any concern about his relationship to God or to any other kind of divine transcendence. For all of them the meaning of life seems to be something to be sought in the present rather than in the beyond; and it also seems to be up to each of them to find his own meaning. An existentialist might say of them that their chief concern is to realize an authentic existence in the real world. In the case of the main characters both the search for meaning and the search for integration is, moreover, an essentially lonely one, for most of them, as we saw, live in a kind of isolation. Their search for human companionship and understanding is also further complicated by the fact that most of them suffer from some anxiety or prejudice which prevents their relating to others in a normal way. All of these things about them cause us to feel them closely akin to characters we have met in contemporary works. They seem modern, too, in that they are individuals rather than types or representatives of general human qualities or attitudes as so many characters in literature were prior to 1830.

As an essentially autodidactic person Ludwig had little systematic knowledge of philosophy, but his stories nevertheless reflect a philosophical point of view concerning the nature of reality. What first strikes us about it is its seeming ambiguity. His attempts to give the reader the impression of an objective reality would seem on the one hand to presuppose a realistic theory of knowledge, in the sense that positing such a reality seems to reflect the belief that the objects revealed or inferred by sense-perception actually exist independently of being perceived or known. The manner in which the characters experience this same reality, however, particularly in the stories from *Maria* on, seems to reflect a totally different view, for what they experience is actually only an impression of reality. This manner of representing reality as something which is both objective and subjective is one of the most important affinities between Ludwig and the other German writers of his day whom we think of as realists, and it also marks him as a forerunner of the writers of our own day.

This ambivalent view of reality is perforce reflected in the style of the stories. In pursuit of his aim of verisimilitude Ludwig accommodated the language in the dialogue passages to the background and temperament of his characters; and since he, as narrator, did not speak the same kind of language, dialogue and narrative differ somewhat in level. This naturally posed a problem in light of his higher aim of imparting to his works aesthetic beauty and poetic content. His method of preserving what he considered to be the necessary artistic tone was to maintain in the narrative passages a fairly high poetic level and to eschew in the dialogue passages anything which might be interpreted as vulgar or common. Even in the sequences in which he identifies himself most closely with his characters we sense a difference between his language and theirs which makes us at all times aware of his controlling presence.

As we follow Ludwig's development from his romantic beginnings in his first stories, through the experiments in techniques and subject matter, to the successful stories after *Maria*, we are able to appreciate more fully how representative he was of the new ways of looking at reality and the new methods of representing reality in art which were being developed in his day. For the account of his evolution as a writer of fiction is actually a kind of history in miniature of the main current of German fiction as it developed from romanticism toward realism in the years following Goethe's death. He offers us, moreover, not only examples of what was then happening in fiction, but also a critical account of the new developments by one who was actively participating in them.

For those interested in the theory of genres Ludwig's later stories have added interest in that they also exemplify the evolution which took place in fiction as a consequence of the increasing use of the dramatic method of characterization. For even though fictional works contained dialogue long before the nineteenth century, it was not until then that the dramatic element really became an important element in narrative writing. Many nineteenth century narrative works accordingly strike us as hybrid types, and to the extent that Ludwig's later stories also exemplify this kind of "cross-breeding" they may be cited as constituting in this respect, too, a kind of epitome of the new developments in German fiction in his day.

In Ludwig's last four stories we find many qualities which we normally associate with realistic writing; yet if we apply in judging them as realistic works the standards of Lukács or even those of Auerbach in his chapter on *Germinie Lacerteux*, they fail to qualify, for they neither reflect contemporary reality nor make us conscious of the social process as these critics thought realistic works should. Indeed, they do not reflect political, social, and economic problems at all. On the other hand, the exciting depth-psychological view of character which we find in them makes them quite impressive examples of psychological realism and even of the kind of psychological realism which we find in *Madame Bovary*, which Auerbach cites, and even largely for this reason, as one of the most important examples of represented reality in nineteenth century literature!

The confusion which we experience in attempting to talk about Ludwig's stories as examples of realistic writing is proof that the term "realism" and its derivatives are still in need of more refined definition if they are to become truly useful to us for discussing what happened in literature during the age of realism. To provide the basis for this more refined definition we must first attempt to reach a fuller understanding than we presently have of the individual works written during the period between 1830 and 1880, for since both the theory and practice of realistic writing varied not only from decade to decade and from author to author, but even from work to work during that long span of years, we shall not be able to describe adequately what happened to literature during that time until we have first studied closely as examples of represented reality all of the major works which appeared between 1830 and 1880. Two very fine examples of the kind of study we need are Walter Silz's book, *Realism and Reality: Studies in the German Novelle of Poetic Realism*, and Richard Brinkmann's study *Wirklichkeit und Illusion*, but much work remains to be done.

Since my own study discusses only the narrative works of one writer it perforce does not contribute much toward clearing up the present confusion in terminology. It does show, however, what "realism" meant in theory and practice to a writer who in many important ways was representative of the new developments in literature in his day; and it also suggests a common sense method of approaching the problem of realism, one, incidentally, which is not unlike that proposed by Fritz Martini in his recently published survey of the critical literature on the problem of realism.[1] I should like to see similar studies on Immermann, Auerbach, Droste-Hülshoff, Stifter, Raabe, Freytag, Spielhagen, Keller, Storm, Fontane, and others, for not until we have detailed analyses of their works as examples of "realism" will we have the necessary basis for studying the phenomenon of literary realism in German literature in the only fruitful way: by considering it as a process of shifting conceptions of form and of changing attitudes toward reality between 1830 and 1880.

In discussing Ludwig's fictional works from these two points of view I have used mainly the tools of the literary historian, but I have also attempted to call attention to the larger implications of the problem, both by considering the stories as reflections of a philosophical point of view concerning the nature of reality and of being and by pointing out, in the case of the stories from *Maria* on, how the composition was affected by what Ludwig learned about the problem of representing reality in the visual arts from the painters and sculptors whom he met in Dresden. This connection between literature and the fine arts during the age of realism has, I feel, been far too little investigated, and a closer study of it would lead, I am sure, to many valuable insights which I can only suggest here. For it is apparent, even to a casual observer, that painters, sculptors, and architects were pursuing in their respective fields the same objectives which Ludwig and so many other contemporary writers were attempting to realize in their dramas and fictional works.

By the time Ludwig's first story had appeared the earlier concerns of architects, the palace and the church, had been replaced by new and more practical problems. The great architect Karl Friedrich Schinkel expresses this new sense of practical realities when he remarks in the 1820's that for him and his contemporaries

Überfahrt am Loreleyfelsen                    Oswald Achenbach

Überfahrt am Schreckenstein                                      Ludwig Richter the sense of the monumental is a thing of the past. It is reflected, too, in many of his structures. Even his famous *Schloss Glienicke* (1826) and his *Charlottenhof* (1829) were not conceived as palaces in the old sense of the term, but as residences of comfortable proportions; and in 1827 this versatile architect designed the first modern department store. Elsewhere in Europe, as we know, factories arose during the 1830's, and in the designs and plans for these the architects attempted to preserve the same kind of balance between functionalism and aesthetic appeal which the early realists were trying to achieve between real and ideal content.

In German painting in Ludwig's day we can observe the same kind of development from a romantic to a more realistic manner of representing reality that we noted in his narrative works, and in the paintings, too, we see realism developing by gradual stages out of romanticism. By the time Gustave Courbet had given a name to the realistic movement in art in 1855 a number of painters in Germany had already begun to draw their subject matter from everyday reality and even to focus, as Courbet did, on its humbler aspects. The foremost representative of realism in painting is Wilhelm Leibl, who was the most famous of Courbet's disciples in Germany. The subjects of his best known works are all humble individuals, peasants, tradesmen, people from the rank and file of humanity, and all are represented with a high degree of faithfulness to reality and a minimum of idealization.

One can gain an idea of the full scope of the changes which occurred in the manner of representing reality in painting between 1830 and 1860 by comparing two paintings such as Ludwig Richter's *Überfahrt am Schreckenstein* (1837) and Oswald Achenbach's *Überfahrt am Loreleyfelsen* (1862), for in these two versions of the same theme a number of things stand out which at once indicate the shift in values which took place during that interval. To make my point clear I need point out only a few obvious differences in content. In Richter's picture what first strikes us is that the figures represent both various phases of human life and various human attitudes, experiences, and activities. We have representatives of childhood, youth, maturity, and old age; and we also have a poet, a musician, a wanderer, a ferryman, and a pair of lovers. One has the impression that these people have not known one another before, for they seem self-contained, as people do when thrown together in a public conveyance; but as they are ferried across the Rhine they all share a common experience, nevertheless, for all of them, we note, are listening to the music of the old harpist. This unifying experience imparts to the painting as a whole a feeling of unity which we might describe as a unity of tone-feeling. This mood is, of course, enhanced by other elements in the picture such as the romantic castle on the hill-top, the new moon, and the haze on the distant hills. The fact that it is evening, and also the fact that the ferryman is an old man seem to indicate that Richter wished to endow his picture with a kind of mythological significance, for as he portrays it the situation in which these people find themselves is somehow symbolic of human life as a whole, which has often been likened to a passage between two shores. As one studies the painting it thus becomes evident that the individual figures and the situation are symbolic of something beyond themselves, and it also becomes clear that the symbolic significance of the people in the picture is more important than their real identity. They are significant because of what they represent, not because of what they are.

Achenbach's picture, on the other hand, shows us only a group of people being ferried across the Rhine, nothing more. No common experience establishes a feeling of rapport among them, and there is also nothing about them to suggest that they represent anything beyond themselves. The only purpose of their journey seems to be to reach the other side of the river. In contrast to Richter's painting, too, we note that everything is portrayed with much greater faithfulness to actual reality. We see faults in the rocks, and the river has a current. It would be but a step from a picture such as this to the daguerreotype. But, significantly, the picture is not a daguerreotype; it is a composed landscape which Achenbach intended the spectator to experience as a work of art, and it even has a certain measure of *Stimmung*. Verisimilitude, however, was obviously a more important concern for Achenbach than it was for Richter thirty-five years earlier. He seems indeed to have pursued it at the expense of ideal content, for the picture certainly means little beyond itself. In drawing his subject matter from everyday life Achenbach faced, we see, the same kind of problem which Ludwig encountered in attempting to make value experiences of his stories of everyday life, for Achenbach, too, wished to offer not only a convincing illusion of real life, but also the kind of ordered and harmoniously arranged image which provides aesthetic enjoyment. In the case of both Achenbach's painting and of Ludwig's stories we might perhaps best describe the final product as a heightened, or poetically adjusted vision of reality.

Ludwig formulates this as an aim for contemporary fiction when he remarks in the *Romanstudien* (*S*, VI, 75) that the goal of the narrative writer should always be "Poesie der Wirklichkeit, die nackten Stellen des Lebens überblumend, die an sich poetischen nicht über die Wahrscheinlichkeit hinausgehoben." His own imitations of reality in pursuit of this aim resulted neither in truth nor in reality, as we saw, but in what we might call plausibility. In light of his conviction that the work of art must always be wrought in such a way as to produce a kind of catharsis they could not indeed have turned out otherwise. It would not be stretching the term too far to describe his stories as little myths about human life and experience, for that is what they really are.

Ludwig's contemporary Theodor Fontane held a far less restrictive view of realism than Auerbach or Lukács, and he also had great sympathy and understanding for what his contemporaries were trying to achieve in literature. Perhaps it is for this reason that we find in his writings[2] a better formulation than in the *Romanstudien* of what Ludwig meant by "Poetischer Realismus." I can think of no more fitting way of closing my study than by citing his remarks here, both as a description of Ludwig's aim as a writer of fiction and as a summation of his achievements in the best of his fictional works: "Was soll ein Roman? Er soll uns, unter Vermeidung alles Uebertriebenen und Hässlichen, eine Geschichte erzählen, an die wir glauben. Er soll zu unserer Phantasie und unserem Herzen sprechen, Anregung geben ohne aufzuregen; er soll uns eine Welt der Fiktion auf Augenblicke als eine Welt der Wirklichkeit erscheinen, soll uns weinen und lachen, hoffen und fürchten, am Schluss aber empfinden lassen, teils unter lieben und angenehmen, teils unter charactervollen und interessanten Menschen gelebt zu haben, deren Umgang uns schöne Stunden bereitete, uns förderte, klärte und belehrte."

# NOTES

KEY TO ABBREVIATIONS

S     *Otto Ludwigs gesammelte Schriften*, ed. A. Stern and E. Schmidt. 6 vols. Leipzig, 1891.
W     *Otto Ludwig Werke*, ed. P. Merker and others. 6 vols. München und Leipzig, 1912-1922.
Vogtherr   *Otto Ludwig Briefe*, ed. K. Vogtherr. Weimar, 1935.
OLK   *Otto Ludwig-Kalender. Jahrbuch des Otto Ludwig-Vereins*, ed. W. Greiner. Weimar, 1929-1942.
DVLG   *Deutsche Vierteljahresschrift für Literaturwissenschaft und Geistesgeschichte*
ZfdP   *Zeitschrift für deutsche Philologie*
SW   G. W. F. Hegel, *Sämtliche Werke. Jubiläumsausgabe*. Stuttgart, 1949.
Minor   *Fr. Schlegel. Seine prosaischen Jugendschriften*, ed, J. Minor. Wien, 1882.

## INTRODUCTION

1. *S*, VI, 156.
2. *Ibid.*
3. The one comprehensive study is that of Gaston Raphäel, *Otto Ludwig. Ses Théories et ses Oeuvres romanesques*. Paris, 1919-1920. As Raphaël's subtitle indicates, however, his main concern is to compare practice, as exemplified in the tales, with theory as set forth in the *Romanstudien*.
4. Julian Schmidt. *Geschichte der deutschen Literatur von Leibniz bis auf unsere Zeit*, V, 245.
5. *Ibid.*
6. In his articles in *Die Grenzboten*, 1841-60, and in his history of literature cited above.
7. Since the appearance of *Aufriss der deutschen Literaturgeschichte* by H. A. Korff and W. Linden (Leipzig und Berlin, 1930) it has become customary to designate this period as the "Age of Realism." See also: Alfred Zäch, "Der Realismus," in *Deutsche Literaturgeschichte in Grundzügen*, ed. J. Boesch, Bern, 1946; and H. O. Burger, "Der Realismus des neunzehnten Jahrhunderts, "in *Annalen der deutschen Literatur. Geschichte der deutschen Literatur von den Anfängen bis zur Gegenwart*, Stuttgart, 1951-52.
8. Brinkmann is right in pointing out that these critics have tended to overemphasize empirical content in their discussions of the works of the realists, but the fact that they are not all guilty to the same degree makes it seem unjust to lump them all together as he does. He also seems unduly harsh toward Lukács, as Gerhard Kaiser has pointed out in his article, "Um eine Neubegründung des Realismusbegriffs," *ZfdP*, 77 (1958), 164 ff.
9. For the critical reaction to Brinkmann's study see particularly: G.

Kaiser, *Op. cit.*; F. Koch, "Zur Kunst der Interpretation," *ZfdP*, 77 (1958), 407-422: and the very negative review by Renate Heuer, *Euphorion*, 53 (1959), 467-474.
10. In "Deutsche Literatur in der Zeit des 'bürgerlichen Realismus,'" *DVLG*, 34 (1960), 581-666.
11. These remarks were quoted in *Newsweek*, March 10, 1957.

## CHAPTER I

1. This group, we now know, also included Johanna Friederike Conrad, Ludwig's *Jugendgeliebte*, an attractive girl with a lovely soprano voice who was unknown to his early biographers. In the summer of 1834, which was one of the young Ludwig's happiest and most productive, the couple, who were inseparable, were looked upon as engaged. A rival came along soon after this, however, and since he was both more worldly and more affluent than Ludwig he succeeded at last in sweeping Johanna off her feet. This shattering experience doubtless explains the note of melancholy and pessimism which we feel in so many of the lyric poems which Ludwig wrote during this period. For a full account of this romance see: Karl Kley, "Johanna Friederike Conrad, die Eisfelder Jugendgeliebte Otto Ludwigs," *OLK* (1931), 37-51.
2. Heinrich Laube, G. Kühne, and Hermann Marggraff were all living then in Leipzig, and one of the most important of the "Young German" periodicals, *Die Zeitung für die elegante Welt*, was being published there.
3. He describes these symptoms in a letter to J. G. Buck, *Vogtherr*, I, 46.
4. See my article, "Otto Ludwig as a Lyric Poet," *Tennessee Studies in Literature*, V (1960), 43-50.
5. H. H. Borcherdt gives an account of the genesis of the story in his introduction in *W*, I, xxiv-xxvii.
6. As Marianne Thalmann points out in her article, "E. T. A. Hoffmanns Wirklichkeitsmärchen," *Journal of English and Germanic Philology*, LI (1952), 473-491.
7. See Marianne Thalmann, *Op. cit.*, and my article, "E. T. A. Hoffmann as Psychological Realist. A Study of *Meister Floh*," *Monatshefte*, XLVII (1955), 65-80.
8. I refer to the dream-sequence in the seventh adventure, which is the culminating moment of the tale. At one point in the conversation which takes place the flea-hero deplores the narrowness of outlook which he has observed in human beings and cites as an example in point Peregrinus' own view of the strange adventures in which he has become involved. He reprimands Peregrinus here for calling things "wondrous" simply because he is unable to understand them in terms of his own limited notions of causality.
9. The main episodes are from a comedy-fragment which Ludwig planned to entitle *Das Hofgesinde*. Structurally the two works are also similar, for *Das Hausgesinde*, too, is little more than a loosely connected series of tableaux.
10. "Soviel ich bis jetzt aus mir klug geworden," he writes at this time, "ist es das poetische Element in der Musik, das mich zu dieser gezogen hat, und ich werde wohl nur in den musikalischen Gattungen, die auf jene gegründet, etwas zu leisten vermögen." Gerhard Glaser, "Otto Ludwig als Musiker," *OLK* (1932), 99.
11. The musical projects never became realities. The few pieces which he composed in Leipzig during the spring and fall of 1840 were the last of his musical works. For a complete list of these see Gerhard Glaser, "Otto Ludwig als Musiker," *OLK* (1932), 77-104.

## CHAPTER II

1. In German the terms are "der rechte Verstand" and "der linke Verstand."
2. We find an eloquent commentary on the literary scene and a strong statement of Ludwig's attitude toward "Young Germany" in his letter of March 2-3, 1840, to Carl Schaller: "Im Allgemeinen hat mich der Ton, der jetzt in der Schriftstellerwelt herrscht, verletzt, dieses von aller Pietät verlassene Wesen! Jeder Gelbschnabel will dem Poeten vorschreiben, wie er dichten soll und hat er den Muth, er selbst zu sein, so entgeht er den scheusslichsten Persönlichkeiten nicht. Wer mag da seine Kräfte, sein Leben, sein Glück, seine Gesundheit riskieren! Thue dir selbst genug ist das wahre, innere Gesetz, dem wir möglichst nah kommen sollen. Und hat man es nach Kräften gethan, nicht Gesundheit, nicht irdisches Wohl zu hoch geachtet, sie auf dem Altar zu opfern, und es kommen Menschen, die selbst nichts produzieren, als Kritik in einer zuckerwasserverschwemmten, characterlosen Prosa, die ich nur einen Ohren- und Sinnenkitzel ohne tiefern Sinn, ja ohne praktischen Werth, denn man bringts nicht so weit, nur heraus zu lesen, was sie wohl mögen gewollt haben, nennen kann und giessen ihr Gift darüber hin. Und das Publikum hat einen Geschmack daran gefunden, sich auf diesen Oberflächen zu wiegen in der Meinung, es denke und wer weiss, wie tief und die produktiven Autoren über die Achsel anzusehen und sich zu freuen, wenn sie recht gemein heruntergerissen werden. Das ist das junge Deutschland. Lies ihre Schriften; es ist unmöglich einem einen Begriff dieser Tigergrube zu machen..." *Vogtherr*, I, 17-18.
3. See "Otto Ludwigs Stellung zur Revolution von 1848 nach seinen Briefen an Ludwig Ambrunn," *OLK* (1939), 82-92.
4. As Hugo von Kleinmayr has so ably demonstrated in his study, *Welt- und Kunstanschauung des 'Jungen Deutschland.'* Wien, 1930.
5. See *Sämtliche Werke. Jubiläumsausgabe* (Stuttgart, 1949), III, 233, or XI, 60 ff. This edition will be referred to subsequently as *SW*.
6. Thus we read (*SW*, III, 48) that "Die Wahrheit ist Übereinstimmung des Begriffs mit seiner Gegenständlichkeit," or (*SW*, VII, 73) that "Wahrheit in der Philosophie heisst das, dass der Begriff der Realität entspreche."
7. In his *Quarantäne im Irrenhaus* Gustav Kühne speaks of Hegel's philosophy as inaugurating a "revolutionary epoch" in his life. Gutzkow repeatedly mentions Hegel's significance for the development of modern thought, even expressing his admiration in an amusing little *Xenion* in the *Telegraph*, 1841: "Rotteck kam bis zu Kant und Wolfgang Menzel bis Fichte / Doch die Sonne der Zeit ging in Hegel erst auf. / Was die anderen spannen, die knüpften's an Formeln; doch Hegel / Spann von allen zuerst an die Geschichte sein Werk." Heine occasionally pokes fun at his former professor, as in the well-known poem in *Heimkehr* (No. 58), but he also had great respect for his intellect. The other Jungdeutschen also frequently pay tribute to Hegel in their writings. See Kleinmayr, *Op. cit.*, chap. II, "Der Reiz des Lebens," 23-40.
8. Wienbarg's enthusiasm for realism in art led him at times to praise rather mediocre works merely because they were true to life. An example is his praise of Hermann Kretschmar's genre painting, *Zwei Kinder belauschen das Nest einer Henne*, which was exhibited in Hamburg in 1835. Wienbarg's review appears in his *Literarische und kritische Blätter*, 1835, No. 1053, "Die fünfte Hamburger Kunstausstellung," cited by Kleinmayr, *Op. cit.*, 38.
9. T. Mundt, *Allgemeine Literaturgeschichte*, 1846, I, 5, 22, cited by Kleinmayr, *Op. cit.*, 45.
10. Cited by Kleinmayr, *Op. cit.*, 60. It is interesting to note that in dis-

tinguishing as he does here between *Wahrheit* and *Wirklichkeit* Gutzkow is moving away from Hegel's aesthetic outlook.
11. *Unterhaltungen am häuslichen Herd*, Neue Folge, II. Band (1857), 319.
12. See his article, "Die 'Realistischen' Erzähler," *Ibid.*, 270-272.
13. Cited by Kleinmayr, *Op. cit.*, 77.
14. Considered collectively, the writings of the *Jungdeutschen* reflect a large measure of social concern, and this concern inclined them to sympathize with the ideas of Saint-Simon, Louis Blanc, and other social reformers of the day. Although they were sympathetic, however, they never gave their active support to any of these utopian socialist schemes. Nor did they ever become champions of the proletariat as Marx and Engels did. The step from social concern to social action was taken only later, during the days just before 1848, when more radically minded poets actively espoused the cause of political and social revolution.
15. Since the *Jungdeutschen* admitted their aesthetic shortcomings so openly, it seems unfair to judge them as severely from the aesthetic point of view as some critics (including Otto Ludwig) have done.
16. Ludwig later set forth these ideas in his famous essay, "Der Poetische Realismus," *S*, V, 458-462. See also his essay, "Mein Verfahren beim Poetischen Schaffen," *S*, VI, 215-219.
17. *The Complete Works of Samuel Taylor Coleridge*, New York, 1854, IV, *Lectures upon Shakespeare and other Dramatists*, "Shakespeare's Judgement equal to his Genius," 55.
18. This idea reflects the influence of Karl Wilhelm Ferdinand Solger, to whose views on the role of the "Verstand der Phantasie" in poetic creativity Ludwig refers in "Der Poetische Realismus." The poetic world so created becomes, as Ludwig expresses it, "Eine Welt, die in der Mitte steht zwischen der objektiven Wahrheit in den Dingen und dem Gesetze, das unser Geist hineinzulegen gedrungen ist, eine Welt, aus dem, was wir von der wirklichen Welt erkennen, durch das in uns wohnende Gesetz wiedergeboren." *S*, V, 459.
19. The people in the "poetic" world resemble those in the real world in the same manner and to the same degree that its structure corresponds to that of the real world, for they, too, are more "transparent" than real human beings.
20. For a full accont of these influences see: Wilhelm Otto Greiner, *Die ersten Novellen Otto Ludwigs und ihr Verhältnis zu Ludwig Tieck*, Pössneck i. Thüringen, 1903; Hans Heinrich Borcherdt, "Otto Ludwigs Novelle 'Die Emanzipation der Domestiken'" *Abhandlungen zur deutschen Literaturgeschichte. Franz Muncker zum 60. Geburtstag*, Munich, 1916, 162-189; and Siegfried Wünscher-Eisenach, "Otto Ludwigs Jugendnovellen," *OLK* (1936), 43-54.

## CHAPTER III

1. *W*, I, xxxv.
2. *Ibid.*, xxxvi.
3. *Ibid.*, xxxviii.
4. The source, to which Ludwig's attention was doubtless drawn by Wetzstein, was *Theater der Hindus*, 2 vols., Weimar, 1828 and 1831, a metrical translation by O. L. B. Wolff of an English work, *Select Specimens of the Theatre of the Hindus*, translated from Sanskrit by Horace Wayman Wilson, 3 vols., Calcutta, 1827. See Reinhard Wagner, "Zu den drei Sanskritgeschichten in Otto Ludwigs 'Wahrhaftige Geschichte von den drei Wünschen' und ihrer Auswertung durch den Dichter," *OLK* (1937), 96-105.

5. *F. Schlegel. Seine prosaischen Jugendschriften.* ed. J. Minor, Wien, 1882, II, 290 and 296. This title will be referred to subsequently as *Minor*.
6. Because the philosopher's discipline makes him most keenly aware of the disparity between the finite and the infinite, Schlegel regarded philosophy as the "native soil" of irony (Lyceum-Fragment 42, *Minor*, II, 188f.). Among the philosophers Socrates was for him the supreme exponent of irony (*Minor*, II, 198). What seemed to him the basic distinguishing quality in Socratic irony was the unique kind of dissimulation which he found in it, a dissimulation which struck him as being at once completely involuntary and absolutely deliberate. In other respects, too, he found Socratic thought a union of opposites, and because he saw it in this light, as a harmonious fusion of opposites, he regarded it as the supreme expression of the ironic attitude as he understood it.

   Only in the works of the greatest poets of world literature – Homer, Dante, Boccaccio, Shakespeare, Cervantes, Goethe – did Schlegel find the kind of irony which he so admired in Socrates. To characterize this quality he invented the highly imaginative term "transcendental buffoonery," by which he means the ability of the artist to rise at will to a point of vantage from which he can survey the real world, the world of his work, and his own activity as a creative artist with a detachment not unlike that with which the traditional Italian *Buffo* plays a comic part (*Minor*, II, 188f.). The image of the *Buffo* is an admirable device for communicating vividly the idea of poetic irony, for just as the *Buffo* is a de-personalized medium through which another's experience is expressed, namely that of the character whom he plays, so, too, the ironic work is a kind of de-personalized medium for communicating, in abstract form as it were, the essence of the poet's original experience. One might add here that the figure of the *Buffo* is also in keeping with Schlegel's observation in his *Gespräch über die Poesie* that irony is really the representation of the entire "Spiel des Lebens," since in ironic poetry life is considered and represented as *Spiel* (*Minor*, II, 364).
7. For Schlegel, as we see here, creative activity is a retrospective activity. If the artist attempts to create while still too involved with his own feelings, he felt, he lacks the objective distance which he must have in order to separate what is meaningful from what is irrelevant in his experience (*Minor*, II, 187f.).
8. One of the best discussions of irony is Raymond Immerwahr's excellent article, "The Subjectivity or Objectivity of Friedrich Schlegel's Poetic Irony," *Germanic Review*, XXVI (1951), 173-191.


CHAPTER IV

1. The most important critical articles are, in the order of their appearance: Richard Meyer, "Otto Ludwigs 'Maria,'" *Euphorion*, VII (1900), 104-112; Fernand Baldensperger, "Nachträgliches zum Maria-Motiv: le 'motif de Maria' dans le romantisme français," *Euphorion*, VII (1900), 792-95; Ernst Feise, "Zur Quellenfrage zu Otto Ludwigs Roman 'Zwischen Himmel und Erde' und seiner Novelle 'Maria,'" *Euphorion*, XIV (1907), 778-783; Karl Bode, "Zur Quelle von 'Maria' von Otto Ludwig," *Euphorion*, XVI (1909), 166-178; Gaston Raphaël, "Nochmals zur Quelle der 'Maria' von Otto Ludwig," *Euphorion*, XVIII (1911), 167-170; and Karl Reuschel, "Otto Ludwigs 'Maria,'" *Euphorion*, XXIV (1922), 654-658.
2. Karl von Holtei, *Briefe an Ludwig Tieck*, Breslau, 1864, II, 282.
3. Hans H. Borcherdt gives a succinct account of Ludwig's modifications

of the anecdotal material in his introduction to *Maria*, *W*, I, xxxix-xlv
4. "Fast die ganze malerische höhere Technik kann in die dramatische Poesie herübergenommen werden. Die Gruppe mit ihrer Totalwirkung, Mittelperspektive (Linienperspektive), die Haltung. Der Held vorn mit weichen Konturen und reichem Detail, die übrigen Figuren, je weiter zurücktretend, desto schärfer umrissen und weniger detailliert (Luftperspektive). Die Zeichnung der Charaktere. Hier ausser der Korrektheit, der Stil, der Ausdruck, Klarheit der Anordnung der Gruppe... Modellieren, die Rundung und das Heraustreten der Gestalten und Glieder. – Pastoser Farbenauftrag hilft zur Modellierung, der breite Pinsel zum Stile..." *S*, VI, 28.

## CHAPTER V

1. From the plans and sketches for the novels it would seem that Ludwig intended them as epic counterparts to the "problem" dramas on which he was working during the 1840's, *Friedrich II. von Preussen, Charlotte Corday, Die Rechte des Herzens, Die Pfarrrose, Das Fräulein von Scuderi*, and *Der Erbförster*.
2. H. H. Borcherdt gives a full account of the genesis and development of the fragments in his introduction, *W*, III, xxiv-xxv.
3. For this story, which is particularly difficult to date, H. H. Borcherdt has worked out what seems a very reliable *terminus ad quem* in his introduction, *W*, III, 1. The story was published for the first time in 1873 in Otto Janke's *Hausbibliothek*. The manuscript has been lost.

## CHAPTER VI

1. See "Otto Ludwigs Stellung zur Revolution von 1848 nach seinen Briefen an Ludwig Ambrunn," *OLK* (1939), 82-92.
2. *Nachlassschriften Otto Ludwigs*, ed. Moritz Heydrich, I, 77.
3. In Vienna the play was produced by Heinrich Laube, who was then Director of the *Burgtheater*. Laube was as deeply moved as Heydrich had been, and he, too, felt that the play owed its great affective power to the unusual combination of romantic and realistic elements one finds in it. In his account he describes the strange power emanating from it as "...eine realistische Kraft, welche mit Romantik verquickt war." Heinrich Laube, *Das Burgtheater. Ein Beitrag zur deutschen Theatergeschichte*, Leipzig, 1868, 177.
4. I use the term *Dorfnovelle* to designate a fictional work about peasant life which, though close to reality and even realistic to the point of using dialectal forms, is obviously written for a specific purpose by someone who is more sophisticated than the characters he portrays. The term implies thus, as I use it, the employment of environmental details for the purpose of either heightening the picturesque quality of a work or giving it greater authenticity by making it seem more real to the reader. This kind of writing appealed to the contemporary public for two main reasons: some liked it because it took them into new and unfamiliar places, others because it dealt with a way of life which was threatened by the advance of technology.
5. Following Merker's practice in his edition, I have used the modern spelling *Heiteretei* in this chapter.
6. The idea of a child-intermediary seems to have appealed strongly to Ludwig, for he uses it several times in his works. The motive first occurs in a lyric poem, *Zu stille Liebe* (1840), and is repeated in *Die wahrhaftige*

*Geschichte von den drei Wünschen*, *Die Heiteretei*, and *Zwischen Himmel und Erde*.
7. Ludwig mentions these borrowings from reality in a letter to Ambrunn in September 1858. An earlier letter to Ambrunn from the autumn of 1855 discloses that the heroine's nickname also stems from reality: "In oder um Eisfeld hat's einmal eine Person gegeben, vom Volksmund so getauft. Ich habe von dieser nur den Namen, weil er so bezeichnend..."
8. "Auch von den übrigen Personen," he writes to Ambrunn in September 1858, "ist keine ein Eisfelder Porträt, sie sind sämtlich typische Gestalten, von der jede kleine Stadt, fast jedes Dorf individuelle Verwirklichungen aufweisen kann."
9. One of Ludwig's most important models in the use of this technique was without doubt his great idol, Shakespeare, who employs it constantly. In *Hamlet* the time is out of joint not only because of the state of external events, but also, and even essentially, in terms of the overall meaning of the play, because Hamlet himself feels it as being so. In like manner Lear in the scene on the heath feels the world to be as mad as he himself is.
10. I use the term not as employed by its originator, Hans von Wohlzogen, to describe the musical themes identified with certain characters, situations, objects, and emotions in Wagner's operas, but in its later extended meaning, that is, to describe a literary phrase or expression which, as a unit, is charged, as it were, with a particular significance in such a way that it can serve as a formula for recalling previous contexts of experience, thus constituting an excellent device for constructing a highly unified work with maximum economy.
11. The first studies of any scope on Dicken's influence on Otto Ludwig are R. Müller's dissertation, *Otto Ludwigs Erzählungskunst*, Tübingen, 1904-5, and Heinrich Lohre's article, "Otto Ludwig und Dickens," *Archiv für das Studium der neueren Sprachen und Literaturen*, CXXIV (1910), 15-45. Lohre's study, which reflects thorough familiarity with the *Romanstudien*, is on the whole excellent. My only objection is that he seems at times to lose sight of the fact that the *Romanstudien* were written after the narrative works. In 1911 Fritz Lüder's Greifswald dissertation, *Die epischen Werke Otto Ludwigs und ihr Verhältnis zu Charles Dickens*, was published in Leipzig. Unlike Lohre, who emphasized *Die Heiteretei*, and *Zwischen Himmel und Erde*, Lüder bases his comparison on all of Ludwig's narrative works. He finds the first traces of Dickensian influence as early as 1846 in *Das Märchen vom toten Kinde*. Johanna Betz's Frankfort dissertation, *Otto Ludwigs Verhältnis zu den Engländern*, 1929, and Ellis Gummer's chapter on Dickens and Ludwig in his study, *Dickens' Works in Germany: 1837-1937*, Oxford, 1940, 82-93, add little to what we find in the earlier studies of Müller, Lohre, and Lüder.
12. In her study, *Das Leitmotiv in Otto Ludwigs Erzählungen 'Die Heiteretei' und 'Zwischen Himmel und Erde,'* Diss. JHU, 1951, 10, Lotte W. Forest suggests, in view of the fateful consequences of the "spinning" and "weaving" of these Norn-like ladies, that the motives of spinning and weaving as used in this sequence might even be said to have a kind of mythological significance: "...denn die Handlung erinnert...an die Parzen. Somit wird dann das Spinnen und Weben zum Symbol des Schicksalhaften, während der Klatsch das Prinzip der Fama versinnbildlicht."
13. Auerbach mentions his dissatisfaction in a letter to Emanuel Geibel (April 2, 1856): "...Auch ich war mit der Heiterethei nicht zufrieden, sie ist, wie ich schon damals sagte, zu sehr ins Laub geschossen u. hat sich

verbuscht statt zum Stamme zu werden. Das kam aber, weil er [Ludwig] sich zum erstenmal gegenüber dem straffen Drama gehen liess u. zu sehr gehen liess." H. Schneider, "Otto Ludwigs Beziehungen zu Emanuel Geibel," *OLK* (1933), 68.
14. For a discussion of the critical reception in Germany see Merker's introduction, *W*, II, vii-xxv.
15. It is interesting to note that the *Atlantic Monthly* carried a review of the volume in December of the year in which its first issue appeared (I, 256). The reviewer found it "refreshing" to see that German literary taste was gradually becoming "more realistic, pure, and natural, and turning its back on the romantic school of the French."
16. In Scott's novels Ludwig sensed a similar awareness of the importance of the individual. Speaking of Scott's techniques of characterization, he writes (*S*, VI, 97): "...Die handelnden Helden seiner Romane sind die sittlichen Mächte, die Menschen selbst und ihre Leidenschaften und Schicksale, die er nach sittlicher Gewissenhaftigkeit ordnet. Es geht keine Gestalt an den Sitten, an der Zeit zu Grunde, nur an ihrer eignen Schuld. Sie haben eine Willkür und ein Gewissen, sind Menschen, nicht Repräsentanten von Ideen...Es ist jede Person gut oder schlecht in ihrem menschlichen Kerne, nicht als Vertreter einer Zeit oder Partei; sie selbst sind, nicht die Zeit, gut oder böse in ihnen."

## CHAPTER VII

1. For an account of the genesis of the story see the introduction *W*, III, vii-x.
2. An account of the critical reception may be found in *W*, III, X-XIV.
3. Because *Zwischen Himmel und Erde* is so closely written it must be read with great care. Some of the misunderstood passages have been pointed out by Stuart Atkins in his article, "Some misunderstood Passages in Otto Ludwig's *Zwischen Himmel und Erde*," *Monatshefte*, XXXIII (1941), 308-320. See also his "Note on Fritz Nettenmair," *Monatshefte*, XXXI (1939), 349-352. The two best analyses of the story as a whole are those by Hermann Weigand, in his article, "Zu Otto Ludwigs 'Zwischen Himmel und Erde,'" *Monatshefte*, XXXVIII (1946), 385-402, and by Richard Brinkmann, in his study, *Wirklichkeit und Illusion*, Tübingen, 1957, 145-216.
4. Weigand (*Op. cit.*, 387) finds the background much too sketchy, and it also strikes him as strange that the reader is not made aware of the changing seasons. On the other hand, the sketchiness of the background might also be cited as evidence of Ludwig's skill in evoking the illusion of a background by means of a very small number of salient details, for although we see very little of the city in which the action takes place we never doubt that it is there. By keeping background detail at a minimum he is also able to keep the story in better focus by concentrating our attention on the psychological problems which are his main concern.
5. The disorders of both brothers are so well described that, as Weigand points out (*Op. cit.*, 395), we have but to add the terminology of modern psychopathology in order to have case-histories!
6. H. Boeschenstein inclines toward this view in his article, "Zum Aufbau von Otto Ludwigs 'Zwischen Himmel und Erde,'" *Monatshefte*, XXXIV (1942), 343-356.
7. This fact is mentioned by Karl Kley-Eisfeld in his article "'Zwischen Himmel und Erde' und die Heimaterlebnisse Otto Ludwigs," *OLK* (1940), 59-67. See also Kurt Dahinten-Rossleben, "Ein Beitrag zur Quellenfrage von Otto Ludwigs Erzählung 'Zwischen Himmel und Erde,'" *OLK* (1936), 107-109.

## CHAPTER VIII

1. Heinrich Schneider, "Otto Ludwigs Beziehungen zu Emanuel Geibel," *OLK* (1933), 68.
2. "Die Seelen aus meinen Dramenplänen stehen nachts an meinem Bett und fordern ihr Leben von mir. Dem muss ich ein Ende machen. Ich bin zu krank, ich kann den Seelen ihren Leib nicht mehr schaffen." *S*, I, 315.
3. *Otto Ludwigs 'Tiberius Gracchus.' Trauerspiel in fünf Aufzügen aus dem handschriftlichen Nachlass zusammengestellt mit einer Einleitung und einem Faksimile.* hg. F. Richter. Breslau, 1934.
4. *Nachlassschriften Otto Ludwigs von Moritz Heydrich. I. Skizzen und Fragmente.* Halle, 1874; II.*Shakespearestudien*. Halle, 1871.
5. These are included in vols. V and VI of *Otto Ludwigs gesammelte Schriften*, Leipzig, 1891. Vol. V contains the *Shakespearestudien*, vol. VI the *Romanstudien*.
6. The best brief discussion of the content and significance of the *Shakespearestudien* as Shakespeare-criticism is Alfred Schwarz's article, "Otto Ludwig's Shakespeare Criticism," *Perspectives of Criticism*, Cambridge 1950, 85-100.
7. Some of the better studies on the *Romanstudien* are: H. Lohre, *Otto Ludwigs Romanstudien und seine Erzählungspraxis*, Berlin, 1913; F. Kreis, "Begrenzung von Epos und Drama in der Theorie Otto Ludwigs," *Zeitschrift für Aesthetik und allgemeine Kunstwissenschaft*, XIV, 288-296; and Gaston Raphaël, *Otto Ludwig. Ses Théories et ses Oeuvres romanesques*, Paris, 1919-1920.
8. The Swiss scholar, Albert Meyer, comes closest to pointing this out in his recent book, *Die aesthetischen Anschauungen Otto Ludwigs*, Winterthur, 1957, which attempts to reduce to a kind of aesthetic system the critical views expressed in the *Shakespearestudien* and the *Romanstudien*. Meyer's procedure might be described as the reverse of Ludwig's, for where the latter began with detailed analyses of isolated aspects of the various problems of epic and dramatic writing, Meyer proceeds by extracting from the total corpus of analyses the basic axioms which they seem to illustrate. Having stated what he believes these basic axioms to be, he attempts to define in terms of them Ludwig's idea of poetic realism, his ethical outlook, his views on the drama and the novel, and his typology of the literary artist.
9. As an example of the unsatisfactory kind of end-product to which he felt such philosophizing might lead he cites the "philosophical" drama of his own day in Germany (*S*, V, 36): "Wer die dramatische Litteratur der neueren Zeit in Deutschland ins Auge fasst, wird dem üblen Einflusse des zu zeitigen philosophischen Studiums überall beggenen in dem qualitativ und quantitativ ungeheuern Uebergewichte der Intentionen über das künstlerische Handwerk. Die Luft schwirrt von Seelen, die keinen Leib haben."
10. In the *Romanstudien* Ludwig reveals (*S*, VI, 41-42) that for him the first step in the creative process was a vision of his characters in action. Even before he had worked out the plot of *Der Erbförster*, he tells us, he saw in his mind's eye his hero making the gestures which an actor would employ to accompany the lines in the play which establish the hero's basic moods and attitudes: "So sollte man doch gleich die Bestien totschiessen," "Recht muss doch Recht bleiben," and "ich hab Unrecht."
11. Because he believed that there is a difference between artistic truth and historical truth Ludwig permitted the writer many liberties which a historian does not enjoy. In the choice of subject matter he allowed great freedom, insisting that anything "tellable" can be appropriate subject

matter for a writer, provided that it is not depraved or trivial and is related in an agreeable and plausible manner (S, VI, 42); and he also felt that a writer should feel free to represent happenings out of chronological order, if to do so served his higher artistic purpose (S, VI, 100).
12. One of the main advantages of the novel in Ludwig's eyes was that it offers the writer a better opportunity to express the psychological processes which accompany thought and action: "Im Roman ist breiter Raum für die Darstellung und Ausmalung dunkler Vorstellungen, die Denken und Sprechen begleiten und wechselwirkend leiten. Im Romane kann die ganze psychologische Wahrheit dieser Vorgänge sich austoben (S, VI, 73-74)'"
13. We even find a rather intriguing idea for a new type of drama which was suggested to Ludwig by Dicken's novels. For this hybrid form, which he describes as having the same relationship to Dickens' novels as that of a dramatized novel to a narrative drama, he suggests the name *Genredrama* (S, VI, 67-8).
14. Ludwig's principal models in the use of dramatic techniques were, as I mentioned, Dickens and Auerbach, both of whom he praises in the *Romanstudien* as masters in the art of objectifying their characters. In Dickens' novels, however, he found the use of dramatic techniques exaggerated at times and even remarks at one point (S, VI, 66) that Dickens' characters sometimes seem to him more like actors in a play than characters in a narrative work.
15. While stressing the importance of centrality of structure in narrative works Ludwig also emphasizes that the characters should possess an individuality of their own, and that the episodes, too, should stand out clearly. For although he believed that both characters and episodes are only parts of a larger totality, he also felt that within the world of the work each situation should be clearly defined and each character should appear to live his or her own life.
16. A writer possesses the kind of perspective necessary to create such a poetized vision of reality only after a certain lapse of time, Ludwig felt, for only after he has gained a certain distance from the experience which initially inspired his work does he acquire the kind of composure, objectivity, and detachment which enable him to perceive in the real the sort of essential higher meanings which he should communicate through the medium of his created world: "...Was ihn [den Dichter] damals in den Himmel erhob, was ihn vernichtete, ist nun durch die Fassung der Zeit, durch die Übersicht des Ganzen gemildert und verklärt. Im Anfange des durch die Erinnerung neuheraufgerufenen ist das Ende, das Gefühl des Ausganges, am Ende der Anfang – die Schuld – ideal gegenwärtig (S, VI, 40)."

## CONCLUSION

1. Fritz Martini, "Deutsche Literatur in der Zeit des 'bürgerlichen Realismus,'" *DVLG*, 34 (1960), 581-666.
2. Theodor Fontane, *Gesammelte Werke*, 2. Serie, Berlin, 1908, IX, 238-239.

# LIST OF WORKS CONSULTED

### I. PRIMARY SOURCES.
#### LUDWIG'S NARRATIVE AND CRITICAL WORKS.

Shortly after Ludwig's death several of his friends, including Gustav Freytag, Berthold Auerbach, and Moritz Heydrich, met with his widow to make plans for publishing his collected works. It was agreed that Freytag should supervise the preparation of the edition and that it should include from the *Nachlass* whatever works he might deem worthy of publication. Using as his criterion aesthetic value rather than literary historical significance, Freytag selected for inclusion only three works: *Das Fräulein von Scuderi*; one of the versions of the Agnes Bernauer story; and the dramatic fragment, *Tiberius Gracchus*. This first edition of collected works was published in 1870 (Berlin: Janke) in five volumes with a prefatory essay by Freytag.

Ludwig's critical writings were first published by Moritz Heydrich in his two volume edition of the *Nachlassschriften Otto Ludwigs* (Leipzig: Cnobloch, 1871-74). These volumes, preceded by a biographical study, include what Heydrich considered the most important critical studies.

The next edition of the collected works was Adolf Stern's six volume edition, *Otto Ludwigs Gesammelte Schriften* (Leipzig: 1891). Because of changes which Stern made in some of the texts his edition is not very useful for scholarly purposes. Its importance at the time of its appearance was that it made available several unknown poems, dramatic fragments, prose sketches, and critical studies. The biography by Stern in Vol. I is still a standard work.

Viktor Schweitzer's three volume edition, *Otto Ludwigs Werke. Kritisch durchgesehene und erläuterte Ausgabe*, Leipzig: Bibliographisches Institut, 1898, was an attempt to meet the need for a critical edition of Ludwig's main works. Since the texts are based neither on the manuscripts nor on first printings, however, the edition is also inadequate for scholars.

The next edition was that of Adolf Bartels in six volumes, *Otto*

*Ludwigs Werke*, Leipzig: Hesse, 1900. It contains a good biographical sketch, but it unfortunately has printing errors.

In 1911 plans were made for a compendious critical edition to be prepared under the joint editorship of Paul Merker, Hans Heinrich Borcherdt, Expeditus Schmidt, Conrad Höfer, and Oskar Walzel. The edition was to appear in eighteen volumes and to be in two parts The first was to contain the works proper, the major fragments as well as the completed works; and the second was to include the critical writings and diaries. The critical apparatus was to contain all the known variants of the works printed. When completed the edition was to offer the reader not only the opportunity of gaining a better overall impression of Ludwig's achievements as a writer than had previously been possible, but also the fascinating experience of studying his creative processes. Since the number of unpublished works would have filled many more volumes than had been provided for, however, the editors were unfortunately obliged to limit the edition to what they considered to be Ludwig's major works. The first volume of the new edition appeared in 1912 under the title, *Otto Ludwigs Sämtliche Werke. Unter Mitwirkung des Goethe-Schiller Archivs in Verbindung mit Hans H. Borcherdt, Conrad Höfer, Julius Petersen, Expeditus Schmidt, Oskar Walzel, herausgeben von Paul Merker*. Munich, 1912. In 1922 lack of funds made it necessary to suspend work on the edition after only six volumes had appeared. Recently, however, the first part of a seventh volume was published, *Agnes-Bernauer-Dichtungen, I, 1837-1847*, ed. W. Leuschner-Meschke, Berlin: Akademie Verlag, 1961, and it is to be hoped that others will follow.

## II. SECONDARY SOURCES

Over the years numerous studies have appeared which have illuminated the life and works of Ludwig from many different points of view. Some of these, of a biographical nature, have established the relationship between the facts of his life and his works; others have investigated the moral and social attitudes of Ludwig as these are reflected in his works; and still others have dealt with isolated aspects of his work as a creative artist, focusing attention on his musical compositions, his dramas, or his narrative works. I have listed here only those upon which I have drawn in some way in writing my own study; but since all of them were helpful I should like here to acknowledge my indebtedness to all.

## INTRODUCTION

Adam, R. *Der Realismus Otto Ludwigs*. Diss. Münster, 1938.
Auerbach, Erich. *Mimesis*. Bern, 1946.
Becker, George. "Realism: an Essay in Definition." *Modern Language Quarterly*, X, 2 (1949), 184-197.
Berkhout, A. *Biedermeier und Poetischer Realismus*. Amsterdam, 1942.
Bieber, Hugo. *Der Kampf um die Tradition*. Stuttgart, 1928.
Binkley, Robert. *Realism and Nationalism*. New York, 1935.
Borgerhoff, Elbert B. O. "*Réalisme* and Kindred Words: Their Use as Terms of Literary Criticism in the First Half of the Nineteenth Century." *PMLA*, LIII (1938), 837-844.
Brinkmann, Richard. *Wirklichkeit und Illusion*. Tübingen, 1957.
Brüggemann, Fritz. "Der Kampf um die bürgerliche Welt- und Lebensanschauung in der deutschen Literatur des achtzehnten Jahrhunderts." *Deutsche Vierteljahresschrift*, III (1925), 94-127.
Burger, H. O. "Der Realismus des neunzehnten Jahrhunderts." *Annalen der deutschen Literatur. Geschichte der deutschen Literatur von den Anfängen bis zur Gegenwart*. Stuttgart, 1951-52.
Colum, Mary. *From these Roots*. New York, 1938.
David, Claude. "Theodor Fontane et la Crise du Réalisme." *Critique*, 127 (1957), 1011-28.
Davis, Robert G. "The Sense of the Real in English Fiction." *Comparative Literature*, III, 3 (1951), 200-217.
Greiner, M. *Zwischen Biedermeier und Bourgeoisie*. Leipzig, 1953.
Gutzkow, Karl. *Phönix*. Literaturblatt der Frankfurter Zeitung. 1835.
— "Realismus und Idealismus." *Unterhaltungen am häuslichen Herd*. Neue Folge, II (1857), 319-320.
Hatfield, Henry. "Realism in the German Novel." *Comparative Literature*, III, 3 (1951), 234-252.
Höllerer, Walter. *Zwischen Klassik und Moderne*. Stuttgart, 1958.
Houben, Heinrich. *Gutzkow-Funde. Beiträge zur Litteratur- und Kulturgeschichte des neunzehnten Jahrhunderts*. Berlin, 1901.
Ingarden, Roman. *Das literarische Kunstwerk*. Halle, 1931.
Kaiser, G. "Um eine Neubegründung des Realismusbegriffs." *Zeitschrift für deutsche Philologie*, 77 (1958), 161-176.
Kleinmayr, Hugo von. *Welt- und Kunstanschauung des 'Jungen Deutschland*.' Wien/Leipzig, 1930.
Koch, F. *Idee und Wirklichkeit*. Düsseldorf, 1956.
— "Zur Kunst der Interpretation." *Zeitschrift für deutsche Philologie*, 77 (1958), 407-422.
Korff, H. and Linden, W. *Aufriss der deutschen Literaturgeschichte*. Leipzig/Berlin, 1930.
Lempicki, S. von. "Wurzeln und Typen des deutschen Realismus." *Festschrift für Julius Petersen*, 1938.
Levin, Harry. "What is Realism?" *Comparative Literature*, III, 3 (1951). 193-199.
Lovejoy, Arthur O. "'Natur' as Esthetic Norm." *Essays in the History of Ideas*. Baltimore, 1948, 69-77.
Lugowski, Clemens. *Die Form der Individualitäten im Roman*. Berlin, 1932.
Lukács, Georg. *Essays über Realismus*. Berlin, 1948.
— *Deutsche Realisten des neunzehnten Jahrhunderts*. Berlin, 1951.
— *Wider den missverstandenen Realismus*. Hamburg, 1958.
Martini, Fritz. "Deutsche Literatur in der Zeit des 'bürgerlichen Realismus.'" *Deutsche Vierteljahresschrift für Literaturwissenschaft und Geistesgeschichte*, XXXIV (1960), 581-666.

Matthiessen, F. O. *Henry James: The major Phase.* New York, 1944.
Meyer, Richard M. *Die deutsche Literatur des neunzehnten Jahrhunderts.* 2. Aufl. Berlin, 1900.
Müller-Armack, Alfred. *Das Jahrhundert ohne Gott.* Münster, 1948.
Poggioli, Renato. "Realism in Russia." *Comparative Literature,* III, 3 (1951) 253-267.
Routh, H. V. *Towards the Twentieth Century.* Cambridge, 1937.
Salvan, Albert. "L'Essence du Réalisme français." *Comparative Literature,* III, 3 (1951), 218-233.
Schmidt, Julian. *Geschichte der deutschen Literatur von Leibniz bis auf unsere Zeit.* 5 vols. Berlin, 1886-96.
Silz, Walter. *Realism and Reality: Studies in the German Novelle of Poetic Realism.* Univ. of North Carolina Press, 1954.
Stuckert, Franz. "Zur Dichtung des Realismus und des Jahrhundertendes." *Deutsche Vierteljahresschrift für Literaturwissenschaft und Geistesgeschichte,* 19 (1941), 79-136.
Treitschke, H. *Deutsche Geschichte im neunzehnten Jahrhundert,* IV, Berlin, 1889.
Walzel, Oskar. *Die deutsche Literature von Goethes Tod bis zur Gegenwart.* Berlin, 1929.
Watt, Ian. *The Rise of the Novel.* Univ. of California Press, 1959.
Weinberg, Bernard. *French Realism. The Critical Reaction.* 1830-1870. New York, 1937.
Wellek, Rene. "The Concept of Realism in Literary Scholarship." *Neophilologus,* XLV (1961), 1-20.
Zäch, Alfred. "Der Realismus." *Deutsche Literaturgeschichte in Grundzügen.* hg. J. Boesch. Bern, 1946.

# CHAPTER I

## THE DECISION TO BECOME A WRITER.

### DAS HAUSGESINDE

Borcherdt, H. H. Introduction to *Das Hausgesinde, W,* I, xxiv-xxviii.
Greiner, W. *Die ersten Novellen Otto Ludwigs und ihr Verhältnis zu Ludwig Tieck.* Pössneck i. Th., 1903.
Hewitt-Thayer, Harvey. *Hoffmann: Author of the Tales.* Princeton, 1948.
Hoffmann, E. T. A. *Dichtungen und Schriften,* ed. Harich. 15 vols. Weimar, 1924.
Kley, Karl. "Johanna Friederike Conrad. Die Eisfelder Jugendgeliebte Otto Ludwigs." *OLK* (1931), 37-51.
McClain, William, H. "E. T. A. Hoffmann as Psychological Realist: A Study of *Meister Floh.*" *Monatshefte,* XLVII (1955), 65-80.
— "Otto Ludwig as a Lyric Poet." *Tennessee Studies in Literature,* V (1960), 43-50.
Silz, Walter. "The Kinship of Heinrich von Kleist and Otto Ludwig." *PLMA,* XL (1925), 963-873.
Thalmann, Marianne. "E. T. A. Hoffmanns Wirklichkeitsmärchen." *Journal of English and Germanic Philology,* LI (1952), 473-491.
Wünscher-Eisenach, Siegfried. "Otto Ludwigs Jugendnovellen." *OLK* (1936), 43-54.

## CHAPTER II
## A PARODY.
### DIE EMANZIPATION DER DOMESTIKEN

Borcherdt, H. H. Introduction to *Die Emanzipation der Domestiken*, W, I, xxviii-xxxiii.
— "Otto Ludwigs Novelle 'Die Emanzipation der Domestiken.'" *Abhandlungen zur deutschen Literaturgeschichte. Franz Muncker zum 60. Geburtstage*. München, 1916, 162-189.
Greiner, Wilhelm. *Die ersten Novellen Otto Ludwigs und ihr Verhältnis zu Ludwig Tieck*. Pössneck i. Th., 1903.
Gutzkow, Karl. "Die 'Realistischen' Erzähler." *Unterhaltungen am häuslichen Herd*, Neue Folge, II, (1857) Leipzig, 1857, 270-272.
— "Realismus und Idealismus." *Ibid.*, 319-320.
Hegel, Georg Wilhelm Friedrich, *Sämtliche Werke. Jubiläumsausgabe*. 20 vols. Stuttgart, 1949.
Heine, Heinrich. *Sämtliche Werke*. ed. Elster. 7 vols. Leipzig, 1887-1890.
Kleinmayr, Hugo von. *Welt- und Kunstanschauung des Jungen Deutschland*. Wien, 1930.
Mundt, Theodor. *Geschichte der Literatur der Gegenwart*. Berlin, 1842.
Wünscher-Eisenach, Siegfried. "Otto Ludwigs Jugendnovellen." *OLK* (1936), 43-54.

## CHAPTER III
## A FAIRY-TALE FROM EVERYDAY LIFE
### DIE WAHRHAFTIGE GESCHICHTE VON DEN DREI WÜNSCHEN

Borcherdt, H. H. Introduction, *W*, I, xxxiii-xxxix.
Greiner, Wilhelm. *Die ersten Novellen Otto Ludwigs und ihr Verhältnis zu Ludwig Tieck*. Pössneck i. Th., 1903.
Immerwahr, Raymond. "The Subjectivity or Objectivity of Friedrich Schlegel's Poetic Irony." *Germanic Review*, XXVI (1951), 173-191.
Lange, Victor. "Friedrich Schlegel's Literary Criticism." *Comparative Literature*, VII (1955), 289-305.
Minor. J. ed. *Friedrich Schlegel. Seine Prosaischen Jugendschriften*. 2 vols. Wien, 1882.
Schlegel, A. W. and Schlegel, F. *Athenäum*. Reihe Neudrucke Romantischer Seltenheiten. München, 1924.
Wagner, Reinhard. "Die drei Sanskritgeschichten in Otto Ludwigs 'Wahrhaftige Geschichte von den drei Wünschen.'" *OLK* (1937), 96-106.

## CHAPTER IV
## THE TURNING-POINT.
### MARIA

Baldensperger, F. "Nachträgliches zum Mariamotiv: le 'motif de Maria' dans le romantisme français." *Euphorion*, VII (1900), 792-795.
Bode, Karl. "Zur Quelle von 'Maria' von Otto Ludwig," *Euphorion*, XVI (1909), 166-178.
Borcherdt, Hans H. Introduction to *Maria*. *W*, I, xxxix-xlv.

Feise, Ernst. "Zur Quellenfrage von Otto Ludwigs Roman 'Zwischen Himmel und Erde' und seiner Novelle 'Maria.'" *Euphorion*, XIV (1907), 778-783.
Lüder, Fritz. *Die epischen Werke Otto Ludwigs und ihr Verhältnis zu Charles Dickens.* Leipzig, 1910.
Meyer, Richard. "Otto Ludwigs 'Maria'." *Euphorion*, VII (1900), 104-112.
Raphaël, Gaston. "Nochmals zur Quelle der 'Maria' von Otto Ludwig." *Euphorion*, XVIII (1911), 167-170.
Reuschel, Karl. "Otto Ludwigs 'Maria.'" *Euphorion*, XXIV (1922), 654-658.
Silz, Walter. "The Kinship of Heinrich von Kleist and Otto Ludwig." *PMLA*, XL (1925), 863-873.

## CHAPTER V
## *DIE BUSCHNOVELLE*
## AND THE PROSE FRAGMENTS

Borcherdt, H. H. "'Die Buschnovelle.' Ein bisher verschollenes Werk Otto Ludwigs." *Westermanns Monatshefte*, 1912, 96-107.
— Introduction to the prose fragments, *W*, III, xxiii-lvii.

## CHAPTER VI
## TWO SCENES FROM PROVINCIAL LIFE.
## *DIE HEITERETEI* AND *AUS DEM REGEN IN DIE TRAUFE*

Auerbach, Berthold. *Sämtliche Schwarzwälder Dorfgeschichten in zehn Bänden.* Stuttgart, 1884.
Bertz, Johanna. *Otto Ludwigs Verhältnis zu den Engländern.* Diss. Frankfurt, 1929.
Fischer, Bernhard. "Volksgestalten und Volkstümliches bei Otto Ludwig." *OLK* (1931), 70-77.
Forest, Lotte W. *Das Leitmotiv in Otto Ludwigs Erzählungen 'Die Heiteretei' und 'Zwischen Himmel und Erde.'* Diss. Johns Hopkins University. Baltimore, 1951.
Greiner, W. "Otto Ludwigs Thüringer Erlebnisse und die Urbilder seiner Werke im neuen Lichte." *Thüringer Monatsblätter*, XXXIX, 55-58.
Gummer, Ellis. *Dickens' Works in Germany 1837-1937.* Oxford, 1940.
Kley, Karl. "Otto Ludwig-Erinnerungen in Eisfeld." *OLK* (1929), 33-37.
Kurrelmeyer, William. "A Note on Otto Ludwig's *Heiteretei*." *Modern Language Notes*, LXII (1947), 132.
Lohre, Heinrich. "Otto Ludwig und Charles Dickens." *Archiv für das Studium der neueren Sprachen und Literaturen*, CXXIV (1910), 15-45.
Lüder, F. *Die epischen Werke Otto Ludwigs und ihr Verhältnis zu Dickens.* Greifswald, 1911.
Merker, Paul. Introduction to *Die Heiteretei*. W, II, vii-xxviii.
Müller-Ems, R. *Otto Ludwigs Erzählungskunst.* Berlin, 1909.
Pachaly, Paul. *Erläuterungen zu Otto Ludwigs Heiteretei. Königs Erläuterungen zu den Klassikern*, Leipzig, 1927.
Schlösser, Rudolf. "Der Gründermarkt in Otto Ludwigs 'Heiteretei.'" *Euphorion*, XXII (1915), 94-95.
Schrag, Andrew D. *Situationen und Charaktere in der Dorfgeschichte bei Immermann, Auerbach, Ranke und Gotthelf.* Diss. Johns Hopkins Univ., 1908. German Monographs 3.
Walzel, Oskar. *Das Wortkunstwerk*, Leipzig, 1926.

## CHAPTER VII

### ZWISCHEN HIMMEL UND ERDE

Atkins, Stuart. "A Note on Fritz Nettenmair." *Monatshefte*, XXXI (1939), 349-352.
— "Some misunderstood Passages in Otto Ludwigs' *Zwischen Himmel und Erde*." *Monatshefte*, XXXIII (1941), 308-320.
Besch, Lutz. "Die künstlerische Gestaltung der Novelle 'Zwischen Himmel und Erde.'" *Germanisch-romanische Monatsschrift*, XXXI (1943), 19-30.
Böschenstein, H. "Zum Aufbau von Otto Ludwigs *Zwischen Himmel und Erde*." *Monatshefte*, XXXIV (1942), 343-356.
Brinkmann, Richard. *Wirklichkeit und Illusion*. Tübingen, 1957, 145-216.
Dahinten-Rossleben, Kurt. "Ein Beitrag zur Quellenfrage von Otto Ludwigs Erzählung 'Zwischen Himmel und Erde.'" *OLK* (1936), 107-109.
Emonts, Maria. "Zur Technik der Psychologie in der Novelle." *Germanisch-romanische Monatsschrift*, XII (1924), 328-340.
Feise, Ernst. "Zur Quellenfrage von Otto Ludwigs Roman 'Zwischen Himmel und Erde' und seiner Novelle 'Maria'." *Euphorion*, XIV (1907), 778-783.
Forest, Lotte W. *Das Leitmotiv in Otto Ludwigs Erzählungen 'Die Heiteretei' und 'Zwischen Himmel und Erde.'* Diss. Johns Hopkins Univ., Baltimore, 1951.
Kerrinnis, Ursula. *Morphologische Untersuchungen an Otto Ludwigs Erzählung 'Zwischen Himmel und Erde.'* Diss. Bonn, 1949.
Klein, Johannes. *Die deutsche Novelle*. Wiesbaden, 1956. 173-177.
Lüder, Fritz. *Die epischen Werke Otto Ludwigs und ihr Verhältnis zu Dickens*. Greifswald, 1911.
Merker, Paul. Introduction to *Zwischen Himmel und Erde*. W, III, vii-xxii.
Prince, Lawrence M. "Otto Ludwig's 'Zwischen Himmel und Erde' and George Eliot's 'Adam Bede.'" *Dichtung und Deutung. Gedächtenisschrift für Hans M. Wolff*, Bern, 1961, 113-116.
Reuschel, Karl. "Ueber Anfang und Schluss von Otto Ludwigs 'Zwischen Himmel und Erde.'" *Euphorion*, XXIV (1922), 880-884.
Schöneweg, Harald. *Otto Ludwigs Kunstschaffen und Kunstdenken*. Jena, 1941.
Weigand, Hermann. "Zu Otto Ludwigs 'Zwischen Himmel und Erde.'" *Monatshefte*, XXXVIII (1946), 385-402.


## CHAPTER VIII.

### FROM PRACTICE TO THEORY.

### DIE ROMANSTUDIEN

Alt, Karl. "Schillers und Otto Ludwigs aesthetische Grundsätze und Otto Ludwigs Schillerkritik." *Euphorion*, XII (1905), 648-664.
Heydrich, Moritz, hg. *Nachlassschriften Otto Ludwigs*, 2 vols., Leipzig, 1871-74.
Kreis, F. "Begrenzung von Epos und Drama in der Theorie Otto Ludwigs." *Zeitschrift für Aesthetik und allgemeine Kunstwissenschaft*, XIV, 288-296.
Kretzschmar, August. "Erinnerungen an einen Jüngstgeschiedenen." *OLK* (1932), 7-14.
Leuschner-Meschke, Waltraut. "Aus Otto Ludwigs Kunstauffassung." *Wort und Werte. Festschrift für Bruno Markwardt*. Berlin, 1961, 200-213.
Lohre, Heinrich. *Otto Ludwigs Romanstudien und seine Erzählungspraxis. Wissenschaftliche Beilage zum Jahresbericht der zehnten Realschule zu Berlin*. Berlin, 1913.

Meyer, Albert. *Die aesthetischen Anschauungen Otto Ludwigs*. Winterthur, 1957.
Mis, Leon. *Les 'Etudes sur Shakespeare' d' Otto Ludwig*. Paris, 1929.
Müller, Richard. *Zur Erzählungskunst Otto Ludwigs*. Potsdam, 1904.
Raphaël, Gaston. *Otto Ludwig. Ses Théories et ses Oeuvres romanesques*. Paris, 1919-1920.
Richter, Fritz, ed. *Otto Ludwigs 'Tiberius Gracchus.' Trauerspiel in fünf Aufzügen (Fragment) aus dem handschriftlichen Nachlass zusammengestellt mit einer Einleitung und einem Faksimile*. Breslau, 1934.
— "Die Fragmente und Entwürfe zu 'Tiberius Gracchus,'" *OLK* (1935), 59-88.
Schneider, Heinrich. "Otto Ludwigs Beziehungen zu Emanuel Geibel," *OLK* (1933), 64-84.
Schöneweg, Harald. *Otto Ludwigs Kunstschaffen und Kunstdenken*. Jena, 1941.
Schwarz, Alfred. "Otto Ludwig's Shakespeare Criticism." *Perspectives of Criticism*. Cambridge, 1950, 85-100.
Silz, Walter. "Otto Ludwig and the Process of Poetic Creation." *PMLA*, LIV (1939), 860-878.
Wachler, Ernst. *Ueber Otto Ludwigs aesthetische Grundsätze*. Berlin, 1897.

# INDEX

Achenbach, Oswald, 85, 86
Adam, R., 100
*Aesthetische Feldzüge*, 15
Alt, Karl, 104
Ambrunn, Ludwig, 93, 94
*The Arabian Nights*, 21, 22
Atkins, Stuart P., 95, 104
*The Atlantic Monthly*, 95
Auerbach, Berthold, 32, 39, 45, 51, 52, 69, 70, 84, 94, 97, 98, 103
Auerbach, Erich, 5, 83, 87, 100

Baldensperger, Fernand, 92, 102
Balzac, Honoré de, 39
Bartels, Adolf, 98
Bechstein, Ludwig, 13
Becker, George, 100
Berkhout, A., 100
Besch, Lutz, 104
Betz, Johanna, 94, 103
Bieber, Hugo, 100
Binkley, Robert, 100
Blanc, Louis, 91
Boccaccio, 92
Bode, Karl, 92, 102
Boeschenstein, H., 95, 104
Borcherdt, Hans H., 89, 91, 92, 93, 101, 102, 103
Borgerhoff, Elbert B., 100
Brinkmann, Richard, 4-7, 84, 88, 95, 100, 104
Brueghel, Pieter, 11
Brüggemann, Fritz, 100
Buck, J. G., 89
Burger, Heinz O., 88, 100

Carolsfeld, Schnorr von, 16
Cervantes, 92
Coleridge, S. T., 17, 91
Colum, Mary, 100
Cornelius, Peter, 16
Courbet, Gustave, 85
Dahinten-Rossleben, Kurt, 95, 104

Dante Alighieri, 92
David, Claude, 100
Davis, Robert G., 100
Devrient, Eduard, 44
Dickens, Charles, 39, 48-50, 70, 77, 78, 94, 97
*Don Quixote*, 18
*Dorfnovelle*, 45, 51-52, 93
Droste-Hülshoff, Annette von, 51, 84
Dürer, Albrecht, 16

Eliot, George, 39, 70, 77, 78
Emonts, Maria, 104
Engels, Friedrich, 91

Feise, Ernst, 92, 103, 104
Feuerbach, Ludwig, 63
Fischer, Bernhard, 103
Fontane, Theodor, 84, 87, 97
Forest, Lotte W., 94, 103, 104
Fourier, François, 14
Freytag, Gustav, 45, 69, 84, 98

Geibel, Emanuel, 69, 94
Glaser, Gerhard, 89
Goethe, J. W. von, 6, 18, 35, 48, 65, 76, 92
Gothic Romances, 18
Gotthelf, Jeremias, 39, 51, 70
Greiner, M., 100
Greiner, Wilhelm O., 91, 100, 101, 102, 103
Grillparzer, Franz, 5, 6, 18
Gummer, Ellis, 94, 103
Gutzkow, Karl, 13, 16, 67, 90, 91, 100, 102

Hatfield, Henry, 100
Hauff, Wilhelm, 18
Hebbel, Friedrich, 39
Hegel, Georg W., 15, 16, 90, 102
Heine, Heinrich, 90, 102
Herder, J. G., 3

Hesse, Hermann, 68
Heuer, Renate, 89
Hewitt-Thayer, Harvey, 101
Heydrich, Moritz, 44, 70, 93, 96, 98, 104
Höfer, Conrad, 99
Hoffmann, E. T. A., 10, 11, 24, 34, 101
Höllerer, Walter, 100
Holtei, Karl von, 92
Homer, 92
Houben, Heinrich, 100

Immermann, Karl, 39, 51, 52, 84
Immerwahr, Raymond, 92, 102
Ingarden, Roman, 100
Irony, 25-26, 92

*Junges Deutschland*, 8, 13, 14, 15, 16, 17, 76, 90, 91

Kafka, Franz, 68
Kaiser, G., 88, 100
Keller, Gottfried, 70, 84
Kerrinnis, Ursula, 104
Keyserling, Eduard von, 5, 6
Kindermann, Hans, 5
Klein, Johannes, 104
Kleinmayr, Hugo von, 90, 91, 100, 102
Kleist, Heinrich von, 18, 34
Kley (Kley-Eisfeld), Karl, 89, 95, 101, 103
Koch, Fritz, 88, 100
Korff, Heinrich A., 88, 100
Kreis, F., 96, 104
Kretschmar, Hermann, 90
Kretzschmar, August, 104
Kühne, Gustav, 89, 90
Kunstmärchen, 10, 25, 40, 41
Kurrelmeyer, William, 103

Lange, Victor, 102
Laube, Heinrich, 13, 89, 93
Left-wing Hegelians, 15
Leibl, Wilhelm, 85
*Leitmotiv*, 48-50, 61-63, 94
Lempicki, S. von, 100
Lessing, G. E., 3
Leuschner-Meschke, Waltraut, 99, 104
Levin, Harry, 100
Linden, W., 88, 100
Liszt, Franz, 8
Lohre, Heinrich, 94, 96, 103, 104
Lortzing, Albert, 8
Lovejoy, Arthur O., 100
Lüder, Fritz, 94, 103, 104

Ludwig, Otto, Biographical references, 8-9, 12, 13, 21, 38, 44-45, 69-70, 89, 90, 91
Ludwig, Otto, Works cited:
  *Aus dem Regen in die Traufe*, 12, 52-56, 79, 80
  *Aus einem alten Schulmeisterleben*, 40-41
  *Die Buschnovelle*, 38-39
  *Charlotte Corday*, 93
  *Die Buschnovelle*, 38-39
  *Charlotte Corday*, 93
  *Die Emanzipation der Domestiken*, 13-20, 79, 90-91, 102
  *Der Engel von Augsburg* (Agnes Bernauer), 45, 99
  *Der Erbförster*, 44, 93, 96
  *Das Fräulein von Scuderi*, 93, 98
  *Friedrich II. von Preussen*, 93
  *Die Geschwister*, 8
  *Das Hausgesinde*, 8-12, 18, 19, 79, 89, 101
  *Die Heiteretei*, 12, 37, 44-52, 79, 80, 93-95, 103
  *Das Hofgesinde*, 89
  *Der Kandidat* (*Der Apostel*), 40
  *Klaus und Klajus*, 40, 41, 42
  *Die Köhlerin*, 8
  *Die Makkabäer*, 45
  *Das Märchen vom toten Kinde*, 40, 41-42, 93
  *Maria*, 30-37, 39, 67, 79, 82, 83, 84, 92-93, 102-103
  *Der neue Don Quixote*, 40
  *Die neue Undine*, 40
  *Die Pfarrrose*, 93
  *Die Rechte des Herzens*, 93
  *Romanstudien*, 1, 3, 33, 48, 51, 57, 66, 69-78, 80, 81, 87, 96-97, 104-105
  *Shakespearestudien*, 70, 71, 81, 96
  *Thüringer Naturen. Charakter- und Sittenbilder in Erzählungen von Otto Ludwig*, 52
  *Tiberius Gracchus*, 70, 96, 98
  *Die wahrhaftige Geschichte von den drei Wünschen*, 21-29, 79, 91-92, 93-94, 102
  *Zwischen Himmel und Erde*, 5, 6, 37, 57-68, 79, 80, 94, 95, 104
Lugowski, Clemens, 5, 100
Lukács, Georg, 5, 7, 83, 88, 100

McClain, William H., 89, 101
Mann, Thomas, 68
*Märchen*, 10, 24, 25, 39

107

Marggraff, Hermann, 89
Martini, Fritz, 7, 84, 89, 97, 100
Marx, Karl, 91
Matthiessen, F. O., 101
Mendelssohn, Felix, 8
Merker, Paul, 88, 93, 95, 99, 103, 104
Meyer, Albert, 96, 105
Meyer, Richard M., 5, 92, 101, 103
Minor, J., 92, 102
Mis, Leon, 105
*Die Montagsgesellschaft*, 44
Mozart, Wolfgang A., 10
Müller (Müller-Ems), R., 94, 103, 105
Müller-Armack, Alfred, 101
Mundt, Theodor, 13, 16, 90, 102

Nazarenes, 16
Novalis, Friedrich, 34
Nussberg, Max, 5

Pachaly, Paul, 103
*Poetischer Realismus*, 1, 3-4, 17-18, 76-78, 86-87, 91
Poggioli, Renato, 101
Price, Lawrence M., 104

Raabe, Wilhelm, 84
Raphaël, 16
Raphaël, Gaston, 88, 92, 96, 103, 105
Realism, Problem of in German literature, 4-7, 83-84, 88, 100-101
Reuschel, Karl, 92, 103, 104
Richter, Fritz, 96, 105
Richter, Jean Paul, 13
Richter, Ludwig, 33, 85-86
Romantic Irony (see Irony)
Routh, H. V., 101
Ruge, Arnold, 16

Saint-Simon, Claude H., 14, 91
Salvan, Albert, 101
Sand, Georges, 13, 39
Schaller, Carl, 90
Schiller, Friedrich, 18, 35, 66, 75, 76
Schinkel, Karl F., 84-85
Schlegel, Friedrich, 25-26, 92, 102
Schlösser, Rudolf, 103
Schmidt, Expeditus, 99
Schmidt, Julian, 3-4, 5, 69, 88, 101

Schneider, Heinrich, 95, 96, 105
Schöneweg, Harald, 104, 105
Schrag, Andrew D., 103
Schumann, Robert, 8
Schwarz, Alfred, 96, 105
Schweizer, Viktor, 98
Scott, Sir Walter, 70, 77, 78, 95
Shakespeare, W., 70, 78, 91, 92, 94, 96
Silz, Walter, 84, 101, 103, 105
Socrates, 92
Solger, Karl W. F., 91
Spielhagen, Friedrich, 84
Stern, Adolf, 5, 70, 88, 98
Stifter, Adelbert, 84
Storm, Theodor, 84
Strauss, David Friedrich, 63
Structure, 2, 7
Stuckert, Franz, 101

Thalmann, Marianne, 89, 101
Tieck, Johann L., 10, 18, 30, 32, 34, 91
Treitschke, H., 101

Vogtherr, Kurt, 89, 90
Von Schwind, Moritz, 33
Vulpius, Christian, August, 18

Wachler, Ernst, 105
Wagner, Reinhard, 91, 102
*Wahrheit* and *Wirklichkeit*, 15-18, 90-91
Waldmüller, Ferdinand, 33
Walzel, Oskar, 5, 49, 99, 101, 103
Warren, Robert Penn, 7
Watt, Ian, 101
Weigand, Hermann, 95, 104
Weinberg, Bernard, 101
Wellek, René, 101
Wetzstein, 21, 30, 31, 91
Wienbarg, Ludolf, 15, 90
Winkler, Emilie, 38, 39, 45
*Wirklichkeit* and *Wahrheit*, 15-18, 90-91
*Wirklichkeitsmärchen*, 10, 24
Wohlzogen, Hans von, 94
Wünscher-Eisenach, Siegfried, 91, 101, 102

Zäch, Alfred, 88, 101

www.ingramcontent.com/pod-product-compliance
Lightning Source LLC
Chambersburg PA
CBHW031321150426
43191CB00005B/273